Endorsements (Affirmations)

I met Ron in December 1984 when I was General Manager of the ~~delphia 76ers. Ron and his family were attending a Fellowship of Christian Athletes (FCA) sponsored event where I was serving as the Master of Ceremonies. Two days later, Ron's wife and mother-in-law were killed in an accident. In 1985, the FCA sponsored the event again. Ron was invited to provide his testimony. He shared how the saving grace of God through Jesus Christ was instrumental in continuing on with life, even though many "WHY" questions regarding his wife's death were never answered. Ron clearly has a strong faith and has much to share from his life experiences where getting off the "WHY" questions and getting onto the "WHAT" questions are so critical. —*Pat Williams, Co-founder of the Orlando Magic, speaker and accomplished author of over 100 books*

I have known Ron Reitz for 50+ years. A devout Christian, he never wavered in his beliefs, regardless of the disaster. When my wife Chris and I lost our son in 2018, I turned to Ron. He told me he was writing a book and he sent me a draft copy. Chris and I sat together and read *Why vs. What;* it inspired many helpful discussions. It showed how deep his faith is and gave us insight as to how he dealt with many challenges in his life. —*Thomas Blackwell, Hatfield, PA; retired elementary teacher, PIAA, and NCAA basketball official*

Based on his own life's experiences of tragedy and loss, Ron Reitz brings to readers a book rich with spiritual insights. Aware of the temptation to dwell on the age-old question of WHY, the author turns the reader to the more helpful question of WHAT. As you travel with Ron through his journey of pain and hope, the readers will find practical suggestions for how the Lord can help turn their tragedies into a life of faith and hope. —*Bishop Neil Irons, The United Methodist Church, Camp Hill, PA*

Ron Reitz's *Why vs. What* is a refreshing perspective on suffering. Ron's voice rises above a cultural milieu that emphasizes fear and victimhood, inviting readers instead to look to God for redemption and restoration. His story is real and relatable, and his storytelling winsome. This book is a guaranteed blessing to all who read it. —*Su Rider, Minister of Generational Discipleship, Halifax UMC, Halifax, PA*

In his book *Why vs. What*, Ron Reitz shares aspects of his life and faith. As you read it, you will experience a gamut of emotions. You will laugh and cry, feel joy and frustration, anger and love. This book can be used in three ways—as a good read, or for personal devotions, or for small group discussions. Enjoy your reading of *Why vs. What*!! —*Rev. George Barto, retired United Methodist Pastor, Camp Hill, PA*

Ron Reitz is the modern day Job. He suffered through almost every stage of his life, yet he found ways to sail above the sea of sorrow. Focusing on faith and not faults, his story is proof that God will take ongoing irritations and make a person's life a pearl. —*Rev. Dale E. Parker, Aldersgate UMC, York, PA*

Ron Reitz is well-qualified to write about viewing life through the lens Of "What is God doing?" versus "Why did this happen?" He has survived the loss of a wife through an accident and a son through suicide. He gracefully accepts situations out of his control and personally struggles with a debilitating disease. Yet, he consistently finds God faithful. His observations will inspire and equip you to journey down life's path, no matter the twists and turns.—*Shirley Brosius, Author and Speaker; Member of Friends of the Heart, CoAuthor of* Turning Guilt Trips into Joy Rides; *Author of* Sisterhood of Faith: 365 Life-Changing Stories about Women Who Made a Difference.

Throughout this book author Ron Reitz is very open, honest and transparent about the joys and struggles of his life. Some of those struggles could be described as "life-shattering." Yet, Ron is equally open, honest and transparent about the faith and trust in God that saw him and his family through those times. May Ron's story inspire and encourage you to discover the "what" when your life seems on the verge of being shattered, too. —*Rev Barry Robison, Harrisburg District Superintendent, Susquehanna Conference, United Methodist Church.*

WHY VS. WHAT

ONE MAN'S SPIRITUAL JOURNEY THROUGH TRAGEDY BY EMBRACING GOD'S PLAN

RON REITZ

SUNBURY
PRESS

Mechanicsburg, PA USA

Published by Sunbury Press, Inc.
Mechanicsburg, Pennsylvania

www.sunburypress.com

For information about special discounts for bulk purchases, please contact Sunbury Press Orders Dept. at (855) 338-8359 or orders@sunburypress.com.

To request one of our authors for speaking engagements or book signings, please contact Sunbury Press Publicity Dept. at publicity@sunburypress.com.

FIRST SUNBURY PRESS EDITION: July 2020

Set in Adobe Garamond | Interior design by Crystal Devine | Cover by Terry Kennedy | Edited by Lawrence Knorr.

Publisher's Cataloging-in-Publication Data
Names: Reitz, Ron, author.
Title: Why vs. What / Ron Reitz.
Description: First trade paperback edition. | Mechanicsburg, PA : Sunbury Press, 2020.
Summary: Certified Lay Minister Ron Reitz attempts to answer the key questions in life from the perspective of a devout Christian.
Identifiers: ISBN 978-1-620064-25-2 (softcover).
Subjects: RELIGION / Christian Living / Death, Grief, Bereavement | RELIGION / Christian Living / Personal Memoirs | RELIGION / Christianity / Methodist.

Product of the United States of America
0 1 1 2 3 5 8 13 21 34 55

Continue the Enlightenment!

Contents

Foreword

My intent in writing this book is for you to see how God helped me grow in a manner that enabled me to face the trials in my life more effectively. By sharing this information, hopefully, we can both further conform to the likeness of God's Son Jesus!

Using my life and the lives of family members and friends as living examples, I am sharing experiences involving the "Why" vs. "What" concept discussed in the INTRODUCTION (Page 1). You will see how God worked through us to rise above the challenges of life, i.e., GOD PROVIDED WISDOM (section at the end of each chapter).

In 2004, shortly after my 29-year-old son Adam was promoted to heaven, my father inspired me to write this book. He said, "Ron, you have had many challenges in your life; you should tell people about these events and how God helped you 'ride the storm' and rise above the issues."

My grandson, Drew Kuhns, is featured in many chapters in this book. Drew has also encouraged me to write this book and said, "Grandpa, it is what it is; you have to tell it like it is!"

The bottom line to all this work is to bring glory to God! I desire to provide thoughts, ideas, and Bible references that will be meaningful and helpful to you as you rise above your life challenges!

This book will be considered a success if, when I am in heaven one day, people will walk up behind me, place their hand on my shoulder and say, "because of your book, *WHY vs. WHAT*, I am in heaven today!"

—Ronald L. Reitz, Author

Introduction

When facing difficult challenges, all kinds of questions surface! Why? What?

"Why" Question Issues

2 Corinthians 4:8 (TLB): "We are pressed on every side by troubles, but not crushed and broken. We are perplexed because we don't know why things happen the way they do, but we don't give up and quit." With the death of my wife and mother-in-law, many "why" questions surfaced for me (now a widower) and our three children (Bryan, Heather, and Adam). I attempted to help them realize that they could live to the age of 100 and not find anyone who can provide acceptable answers to their "why" questions.

We need to recognize that God allows trials into our lives not to destroy us but to improve us. We will suffer greatly if we constantly seek answers to unanswerable "why" questions. This is where our faith and God's grace comes into play, and we try to shift our thinking and focus on "what" can God accomplish through all of this. Note God's promises through Paul in his letter to the Romans 11:36 (TLB): "For everything comes from God alone. Everything lives by His power, and everything is for His power. To Him be glory evermore."

Now, with our focus not just being on "why" did the tragedy happen but more focused on "what" can God accomplish through all this, we can identify "what" question results we should strive to complete. In other words, "what" does God want to accomplish and how can He use us in the process.

Also, since satisfying answers to most "why" questions are not readily available, go to Proverbs 20:24 (TLB): "Since the Lord is directing our steps, why try to understand everything that happens along the way?" Remember Romans 8:28 (TLB), "And we know that all that happens to us is working for our good if we love God and are fitting into His plans."

"What" Question Results

The number and type of "Whats" that can result are limited only by a person's imagination and how much he is willing to "think outside the box." Some examples are memorial funds, donations to a particular cause, building additions, activities that enhance the spreading of the Gospel, scholarships, the creation of "blended" families, etc. Dwell not on "Why" did this happen, but "What" will God accomplish through this? Thus, learn to thrive and rise above the difficult challenges.

All Glory and Praise to God

In the following chapters, I will share my personal and spiritual journey. My purpose is not to bring glory to me or to make my experiences a principle for others but to allow the reader to see the "Why" and "What" in my life and God's marvelous and steadfast work. The Spirit of God is a well of water springing up perpetually fresh. God engineers our circumstances, and we must show unrestrained surrender to Jesus throughout our lives.

1
Acceptance of Christ

When I was between 12-14 years old, most Saturday evenings, my friend Denny Eister and I attended the Youth for Christ Rally held at the Orange Street Elementary School in Northumberland, PA (~170 miles north/west of Philadelphia). Youth for Christ was an international movement with rallies taking place in cities around the globe. On a fall Saturday evening in 1960, I made the most important decision of my life.

On this evening, a young man talked about his relationship with Jesus Christ. He explained by using scripture references that Jesus was God's Son, and He was sent to earth to demonstrate His love for all mankind. If one is willing to accept this love, cast his sins upon God, and accept God into his life in the form of the Holy Spirit, he shall be assured of eternal life in heaven. It is clear from the Holy Bible that a person cannot earn his way into heaven. Promotion into heaven is a gift from God - GRACE. By allowing His Son Jesus to die on the cross and rise to life on the third day, this young man explained, God demonstrated His power over death. In other words, Jesus conquered the grave!

This presentation compelled me to make a conscious decision to say "yes" to Jesus! I wanted to have a similar relationship with Jesus as this young man described. So I accepted my sinful nature and the need for a Savior. I asked God to come into my life in the form of the Holy Spirit, and I accepted Jesus as the "Lord of my life."

The gospel of John 3:16-17 (KJV) states, "For God so loved the world, that He gave His only begotten Son, that whosoever believeth in Him should not perish, but have everlasting life. For God sent not His Son into the world to condemn the world, but that the world through Him might be saved." This assures me that I will spend eternity in heaven if I believe in God, recognize Jesus as God's Son, and accept Jesus as my Savior. I can't "earn" a place in heaven; I am "promoted" to heaven through God's grace.

Today as I look back at my decision, it has become very apparent to me that the most important decision a young person can make is to commit his/her life to Jesus. This commitment can be made by the time the child reaches the age of accountability (i.e., can take responsibility for one's actions/decisions). Once we have this relationship with God through Christ, no one can take it away from us! Also, once we make this commitment, we are ready to begin studying and comprehending God's teachings that are available to us in the Bible!

GOD PROVIDED WISDOM

Romans 3:21-22 (TLB): "But now God has shown us a different way to heaven—not by "being good enough" and trying to keep his laws, but by a new way (though not new, really, for the Scriptures told about it long ago). Now God says he will accept and acquit us—declare us "not guilty"—if we trust Jesus Christ to take away our sins. And we all can be saved in this same way, by coming to Christ, no matter who we are or what we have been like."

Once I made my commitment to God through Christ, I began to recognize the importance of studying the Bible and learning how God wanted to use me. Several important verses came to my attention:

> **Proverbs 3:6** (TLB): "In everything you do, put God first, and he will direct you and crown your efforts with success."
>
> **2 Chronicles 31:5-6** (TLB): "The people responded immediately and generously with the first of their crops and grain, new wine, olive oil, money, and everything else—a tithe of all they owned, as required by law to be given to the Lord their God."

2 John 1:6 (TLB): "If we love God, we will do whatever He tells us to. And he has told us from the very first to love each other."

John 3:16 (KJV): "For God so loved the world, that He gave His only begotten Son, that whosoever believeth in Him should not perish, but have everlasting life."

Philippians 4:13 (KJV): "I can do all things through Christ, which strengthened me."

Matthew 5:16 (KJV): "Let your light so shine before men, that they may see your good works, and glorify your Father which is in heaven."

CHALLENGE:
Which of these verses offers encouragement to you? Why?

2
The Three Ps

My hometown was Sunbury, Pennsylvania, a great place to grow up and experience what I called "The Three Ps." Praising God, Playing Sports, and Pretty Girls.

Praising God: Fortunately, I had parents who cared about each other and regularly showed love toward one another. This provided an example to follow for my future family. It was evident to my siblings and me that my parents were committed to taking us to church and Sunday school. By going to church and Sunday school as a family every Sunday, we were exposed to God's Word and thus encouraged us to be involved in God's work. My commitment to God was very real and very important to me because my parents were excellent role models.

Three of my closest friends, Danny, Gary, and Johnny, also went to church regularly. Each Sunday, we would color coordinate our clothing for the next Sunday by discussing and agreeing to wear the same color tie. Yes, as teenagers, we wore ties to church!

All four of us sang in the church choir and were active in our church Youth Group. Our Youth Group verse was Matthew 5:16 (KJV): "Let your light so shine before men that they may see your good works and glorify your Father who is in heaven." Since my involvement in God's work was very sincere, this verse encouraged me to look for activities that would benefit others. Over the years, this commitment to follow the teachings of the Bible has grown stronger.

With a great deal of focus on my parents in this chapter, I thought it was appropriate to display a picture of them in August 2010 when they celebrated their 70th anniversary.

Playing Sports: Football, basketball, and baseball were my loves. I couldn't wait until the *Sears Roebuck Catalog: Christmas Edition* came out. Every year my Christmas list included many sports-related items.

As a young boy growing up in the 1950s, Friday evenings during football season were very special to me. I would lie in the back seat of my parent's car while they worked on our new home. I listened to WKOK Sunbury for the play-by-play of the Sunbury Owls High School football games. I dreamed that I was Bob Delbaugh, the running back for the Owls. Bob was an awesome, almost larger than life, inspiration to me!

At the young age of eight, I became interested in basketball. Since I didn't have a basketball hoop, I found a piece of stove pipe and nailed it to the basement wall. It was challenging to make baskets with such a small hoop, but it was better than no hoop at all. Every night after saying my prayers, I would fantasize about different sports events where I was the "star."

Pretty Girls: One of my first crushes was a 4th-grade classmate. She was beautiful, and man could she run fast. In "girls catch boys" games that we played at recess, it wasn't hard for her to catch me. I would slow down just enough for her to catch up.

Throughout my junior high years, several girls caught my eye, but only for short periods. It was always interesting to see who would be the next girl that expressed interest in me or the next girl who caught my eye.

As I entered high school (10th grade), my thoughts turned to the idea of finding the right girl to be my long-term girlfriend. From what I understand about today's high school and college youth, long term dating experiences are not the norm.

However, now that I had those turbulent junior high school years behind me, I believed that when I dated a girl, there was an unofficial commitment to each other. Cindy Shumaker was a classmate of mine. Cindy and I began to date in May 1964. Except for approximately one week in the summer of 1965, we were committed to each other until we were married in May 1969.

GOD PROVIDED WISDOM

Matthew 5:16 (KJV): "Let your light so shine before men that they may see your good works and glorify your Father who is in heaven."

God provided, through my mother, an excellent example of how His teachings should be at the focal point of all actions and decisions in life. She strived to let her light shine.

- Virtually every morning when I got out of bed, I found my mother in her favorite chair reading her Bible. She was discussing with God the activities and decisions she had before her.

- Many days during the summer months, she was up at 3–4:00 A.M. cleaning, baking, etc. She said it was cooler at that early morning hour, and thus she got more work accomplished.

- On days when I was home from school, my mother often had hymns, sung by Tennessee Ernie Ford, playing on the stereo. I can still hear her singing, and at times, whistling along with the music.

- Every evening she got on her knees beside her bed, thanking God for His guidance and direction throughout the day.

CHALLENGE:

What examples in your past life can you share that helped direct your ongoing love for the Lord today?

3
Planning a Family Focused on LOVE

When I was in high school and college, my strengths were planning, being organized, and being detail-oriented. I planned out many aspects of my future in great detail. The topics of marriage and family were no exception. In this process, I discovered I should fully rely on God for guidance and direction (an acronym for this process is FROG). This ability to rely on God was possible if I daily spent time in my Bible. I set aside early morning time to read scripture and pray.

Proverbs 3:4-6 (TLB) were excellent verses to keep in front of me as I worked through this process. i.e., "If you want favor with both God and man, and a reputation for good judgment and common sense, then trust the Lord completely; don't ever trust yourself. In everything you do, put God first, and he will direct you and crown your efforts with success."

Below is a summary of how I moved forward when using this process of continued Bible reading and prayer and writing points down that the Holy Spirit brought to my attention:

- Delay marriage until finished with college;

- Become the best Math teacher and coach I could be;

- Three children seemed like the correct number of children;

- Prefer to live in a small rural community;

- Type of family we would be is Christ-like, i.e., strive to live more like Jesus always;

- Our age when the children were out of the house (mid 40's);

- We would adjust to our empty nest by going camping, traveling, working, and worshiping in our church and community to help make disciples for Jesus Christ.

Remember Ephesians 5:25 (TLB): "And you husbands, show the same kind of love to your wives as Christ showed to the Church when he died for her." **Ephesians 5:33b** (TLB): ". . . the wife must see to it that she deeply respects her husband—obeying, praising, and honoring him."

As you can see from the list above, my relationship with my wife was coolly calculated and would require just the right woman. It was the mid-1960's and confusion and uncertainty seemed to be everywhere and created many challenges for us to live as our Christian focus required:

- The escalation of the war in Vietnam;

- The creation of the military lottery used by the U.S. Government to draft persons into the military;

- The invasion of the Beatles (four musicians from England);

- Songs evolving from Elvis ranging from "wild ROCK" to inspirational hymns;

- Continuous merging of our local school districts (i.e., Sunbury & Northumberland School Districts merged to form Shikellamy School District; Mahoney Joint & Trevorton School Districts merged to form Line Mountain School District; Shamokin & Coal Township School Districts merged to form Shamokin School District).

Cindy Shumaker, our sophomore class Secretary, and one of the most beautiful girls in our high school class, was entitled to two tickets to the junior/senior prom. To find a date, she pulled out her yearbook, laid it out on her four-poster bed, and searched its pages for a suitable escort—me? (This decision process to select me was one that would change our lives forever.)

In the high school years following the prom, Cindy and I were inseparable. Cindy was crowned 1965 Shikellamy High School homecoming queen, and I played high school sports and was elected Student Council President. Shortly after high school graduation, Cindy began working as a secretary for a local law firm (Rice & Rice), and I studied secondary education at Bloomsburg State College.

As we continued growing in our love for each other, we shared many common interests through which we were able to demonstrate such love. One such example is excerpted from a letter that Cindy sent to me while I was in college (although the letter contains a lot of humor, it meant a great deal to me. One should never lose sight of the importance and value of such communication in ongoing love/marriage relationships)!

May 1968
Mr. Ronald L. Reitz
Bloomsburg State College
North Hall; Box 1167
Bloomsburg, Pennsylvania 17815
In Re: Love—Love—Love Greetings

Dear Dearest One:
I am writing in reference to the claim which I have on your love—love for what—me! Be it as it may, I am sure you are capable of meeting the requirements for such an honorable position.
I am most happy, as well as very pleased, to tell you of the great love I have for you. I would cross a giant mountain for you, cross the widest river, climb the steepest hill, cook your pheasants, deer, grouse, rabbits, squirrel, scrub your dirtiest floors, wipe your children's noses and drive a thousand miles for you and most of all sit with you through your football, basketball, wrestling, boxing, track, soccer, baseball, and fishing programs . . .
Well Mr. Reitz, if you are willing to accept this position, please call area code 717-286-2856 Thursday evening at 10:00 o'clock PM, May 2, 1968, and give me your answer. May I suggest that the

answer start with the letter Y because if it doesn't, I may have to take immediate action to make you change your mind . . .

In closing, may I submit for your approval, my deepest love and need for you and tell you that I wouldn't know what to ever do without you . . . I love you very-very much.

Lots of Love and Kisses—Your Nutty Honey
L.J.S.cs

P.S. Remember now, I love you!!!!!!!!!!!!!!!!!!!!!!!!!!!!

Cindy and I married May 25, 1969, in a beautiful ceremony, and our first child Bryan was born fifteen months later.

The most important aspect of our married lives together was having the Lord as the number one priority in our lives. Our second priority was to allow Christ-like thoughts and actions to control our lives centered on love for each other and the children that would be given to us to raise.

Now, we need to read the New Testament to get our priorities of life totally in order. The New Testament tells us that the very reason for our being is LOVE. God is love. We were created from love and for love. There is no question about it; God indeed has shown His love to us in many ways. "See how the Father hath loved us," writes John in one of his Epistles. You and I would be here all day if we tried to count how God has bombarded us with the evidence of His love. And if we fully rely on God (FROG) in making our decisions, we will have a better chance to keep our family focused on LOVE!

GOD PROVIDED WISDOM

Proverbs 3:4-6 (TLB): "If you want favor with both God and man, and a reputation for good judgment and common sense, then trust the Lord completely; don't ever trust yourself. In everything you do, put God first, and He will direct you and crown your efforts with success."

When making decisions, Fully Rely On God!

Formula:

- Identify Issue;
- Pray Over Issue;
- Search Bible on Issue;
- Discuss and Pray With Fellow Christians;
- Make Decision; Move Forward; Evaluate;
- Modify if Directed by God; Trust God Totally

CHALLENGE:

Identify a decision that you have before you today. Follow the outline above; it works.

4
Jesus Loves Me!

It was spring 1977, and our family members were growing in size and number. Although we had our share of life challenges in raising our family, many times, those challenges were turned into positive experiences. This was the case in one such experience Cindy had involving our three children when they were singing the beautiful Sunday school song "Jesus Loves Me."

On this particular spring day, Cindy was driving our ideal size family (two boys and one girl) home from a trip to the grocery store. Cows were grazing in the fields that just turned green from the April showers. Birds and bees could be seen everywhere. All aspects of this day had the makings for a fantastic day!

Suddenly, the beautiful scenery, the glorious aroma of the blooming flowers, and the music coming from Cindy and the three kids were interrupted. Adam, who was in his car seat in the back of Mommy's movin' movin' movin' station wagon screamed, "Mommy, Mommy, Mommy, there is a policeman behind us, and his light is going around faster than my toy top!"

Cindy pulled the car off to the side of the road, put on her four-way flashers, and rolled down her window as she frantically searched for her owner's and insurance cards that were located in a glove compartment which was filled with everything but the kitchen sink. As the state trooper walked up to the car, Adam screamed another warning. "Mommy, Mommy, Mommy, the policeman has a gun. Is he going to shoot us?"

The trooper began to make a series of requests and comments: "Your license and insurance cards please. Where are you going in such a hurry? How many children do you have in the car? Do you realize the danger you placed them in?"

Cindy, who always found it easy to talk with anyone in any environment, found this situation challenging! Finally, she began to speak, "Trooper, it is a beautiful day, and my three children and I were enjoying the day and thanking God for His bounty by singing "Jesus Loves Me." I guess the louder we sang, the more excited I got, and the more I pushed the pedal to the metal."

As they were exchanging information, Cindy noticed the trooper's name tag, "Trooper Dubinski." Cindy then addressed the officer by name and thanked him for stopping her before she had an accident.

Trooper Dubinski returned to his car. Using his radio, he learned that Cindy had no prior records of speeding on file. Therefore he decided on a stern warning with emphasis on caring more completely for the safety of her children.

Later that same year (August 1977), the kids and I were loading supplies into our van for use at the annual Sunday school picnic. Soon we would be ready to go over the hills and meadows in God's creation.

Much to our dismay, the huge kettle of chicken corn soup that mommy was making for the Sunday school picnic was not finished; it would take another 45 minutes longer! Mommy asked us to leave for the picnic and tell the ladies at the church that she would be late.

Everything was going as per the adjusted plan when Cindy realized she could not carry the huge kettle of soup to the station wagon. Then she got an idea. She noticed when she came home earlier that afternoon that a Pennsylvania state trooper was sitting in his car at the nearby intersection. So, over to the trooper's car, Cindy went.

Approaching the police car from the back/driver's side, Cindy tapped on the window. The trooper turned reluctantly toward Cindy. With the car window now open, she began to explain her dilemma and to request the trooper's help in carrying the huge kettle out to her station wagon.

At this time, Cindy happened to glance down at the trooper's shirt—there in big, bold letters was his name, Trooper Dubinski. Cindy began to smile, blush, cover her hands over her face and laugh out loud, all at the same time. The trooper looked up at Cindy, and with a huge smile, said, "Yes, Jesus Loves Me!"

Oh, by the way, Trooper Dubinski carried the kettle of soup out to our station wagon.

GOD PROVIDED WISDOM

Psalm 78:4-6a (TLB) reads as follows:
"I will reveal these truths to you so that you can describe these glorious deeds of Jehovah to your children and tell them about the mighty miracles He did. For He gave His laws to Israel and commanded our fathers to teach them to their children so that they, in turn, could teach their children too."

The above passage from Psalm 78 indicates the importance of passing God's teachings on down for the benefit of future generations. One way to do this is through songs. Can you sing while driving and stay focused?

CHALLENGE:
Consider the last time you drove your car/truck. Did you text while driving? Did you place a call or receive a call while driving? Did you adjust the radio dial several times while driving?

If you did any of the above actions while driving, please get a Post-it note and write on it in large print STAY FOCUSED. Then place the note on your steering wheel, and when tempted to do something other than drive, look at the Post-it note and refocus on driving.

5
City of Sunbury Job

The City of Sunbury job and the events of April 11, 1979, to November 11, 1979, provided me with a new perspective regarding one of my father's favorite sayings. My dad used to say, "Ron, if you want to survive in the business world, you have to learn how to step on peoples' toes without messing up the shine on their shoes."

For a clearer understanding of this saying, let me take you back in time to early spring 1979. The Sunbury City Council contacted me regarding a newly created city job titled Work Force Superintendent. I was contacted regarding this position because I had several years of Human Resources experience. They further indicated to me that the technical skills needed to support the maintenance department duties of the city of Sunbury were already in place. What was now needed was a leader who could develop work schedules, work policies, benefits packages, payroll policies, etc., to attain the best results from the workforce going forward. Also, they wanted to be sure all employees are being treated fairly.

My wife and I prayed extensively regarding this opportunity. We felt comfortable through our prayer efforts that this new opportunity was in God's will for our lives. Therefore, I applied and was hired. This very timely process of hiring seemed to be an additional indicator that we were following God's path for our lives.

Unfortunately, this new role was a real bear from the start. The most significant issue was that I misunderstood the technical skill levels of the workforce. My understanding from initial conversations with City Council management personnel was that the employees I would be supervising were competent in the areas of road maintenance, snow removal, flood control, and parks/recreation. However, except for two employees, the remainder of the workforce did not have the necessary skills to perform these jobs. These employees soon made it clear that they felt I would be providing any missing skills. But this was not the case. I was a human resource professional, not a maintenance-oriented expert.

My experiences with the city of Sunbury became very challenging. Disagreements with many different people were frequent. I found myself falling deeper and deeper into a fearful frame of mind. This job was consuming me, awake at night, into work early, and staying at work late. By September 1979, I was close to an emotional breaking point. I had many "why" questions. The most obvious question was, "God, why did you lead me to this job?"

I sat down with my family to discuss my options. After this talk and additional prayer and discussion with my wife, I gave my contract required sixty-day notice to terminate my employment. Once I made the decision, a heavy burden was taken off my shoulders. However, little did I realize how challenging the next several months were going to be with facing unemployment and trying to provide for a family of five with no income. Also, I had to strive to focus on, OK God, "what" do you want to accomplish through all of this?

The main thing I learned from this job experience was, "My needs and God's blessings were a perfect fit; however, I was way too impatient!" As it turned out, I didn't give enough time for things to play out!

For example, my greatest fear in this job all along was the upcoming winter season. Specifically, were the snow removal procedures adequately in place? Were we ready? The snow season in Sunbury extended from December to April. Not only did I have responsibility for the city-owned equipment and city employees, but I also needed to coordinate the efforts of independent drivers hired by the city in times of heavy snow.

Well, during the winter season (December 1979 to April 1980), we did not have one snowfall in the Sunbury area that required the activation of any of the city snow removal equipment! Truly God had it under control!

My needs and God's blessings were a perfect fit! All I needed to do was to have FAITH and TRUST and be patient. God allowed me to make the necessary decisions. I believe that the outcome long term would have been fine either way! God had it all under control. He continued to bless us (Cindy and me) even to the point of providing us both with a job by the beginning of 1980!

GOD PROVIDED WISDOM

The Legend of two Wolves, by Celestial Elf, is an animated video from the Cherokee Nation about two wolves. In the legend, an elderly Cherokee man teaches his grandson about life. "A fight is going on inside me," he says to the boy. "It is a terrible fight, and it is between two wolves. One is evil. He has anger, envy, sorrow, regret, greed, arrogance, self-pity, guilt, resentment, inferiority, lies, false pride, superiority, and ego." He continues, "The other wolf is good. He has joy, peace, love, hope, serenity, humility, kindness, benevolence, empathy, generosity, truth, compassion, and faith. From time to time, this same fight will rage on inside you."

The grandson thinks about it for a minute and then asks his grandfather, "Which wolf will win?"

The grandfather simply replies, "The one you feed."

As I look back on the year 1979, clearly, I was focused on the wrong wolf. I was focused on negative thoughts and feelings ("why" questions) rather than being focused on God's love and promises never to leave nor forsake me. I forgot to search diligently for "what" God wanted to accomplish through all of this.

CHALLENGE:

Are you dealing with any situations in your life where you feel as though you are approaching an emotional breakdown? If so, I challenge you to focus on feeding your mind with God's truths beginning with the following Bible passages; summarize passages in your own words:

- Psalm 44:1-7 _____
- Psalm 46:1-5 _____
- Psalm 95:1-9 _____
- Philippines 4:13 _____
- Romans 5:1-5 _____

6
Down on the Farm

It was now fall 1979. Things were tight financially. I was on the verge of being unemployed and did not qualify for unemployment compensation. My efforts to find employment were falling on deaf ears at every turn in the road. Soon I would have no income. However, Cindy continued to be upbeat and positive. She would continually say we have to have faith and trust in the Lord!

Although we could not afford it, Cindy suggested we go out to lunch at Spess's Restaurant at 4th and Walnut Streets in Sunbury. Once we arrived and were seated in this little, quaint, local neighborhood café, Cindy began to smile broadly, like the cat that just swallowed the canary. She informed me that she contacted the local Tupperware distributorship and signed up to be a Tupperware consultant. She proceeded to tell me how she would receive training, and then be able to conduct home parties, selling this popular line of storage container products. "This effort will take away some of the financial pressure that we are feeling," she said. Cindy then said, "Remember, we need to have faith and trust, and God will show us the way."

From the very beginning, Cindy was successful in this sales position. Within several months she had four sales consultants under her direction, qualifying her to direct her own sales unit. With the birth of her own unit, Cindy had to choose a name for her group. She chose the name: "Faith and Trust." Cindy was very successful at her job because she was a very positive, optimistic, organized person who was willing to take chances. Cindy was a person who loved to smile and laugh. She could strike up a conversation with a lamppost, and she could think and brainstorm outside the box.

Once, Cindy was trying to convince a lady, who lived on a farm, that she should host a Tupperware party in her farm home. Cindy received the impression that she was ashamed of the interior of her home. Not wanting to forgo a potential party, Cindy put her creative mind into gear and suggested a barn party. Why don't we advertise your party by saying, "Tupperware Goes Down on the Farm? You can wait and hold the party in the spring and set up outside. You can use hay bales instead of tables and chairs."

Cindy also said, "You can also have the Tupperware lady receive a quick lesson on hand milking a cow and then have her milk the cow into a large Tupperware storage container. This will provide the guests with a chance to laugh at the girl from the city trying to milk a cow! In terms of prizes for the winners of games and refreshments," Cindy suggested, "You can serve fresh milk and other milk products." Cindy was so successful with this party that she was featured in a Tupperware regional United States magazine.

GOD PROVIDED WISDOM

Mark 2:3-5 (TLB): "Four men arrived carrying a paralyzed man on a stretcher. They couldn't get to Jesus through the crowd, so they dug through the clay roof above his head and lowered the sick man on his stretcher, right down in front of Jesus. When Jesus saw how strongly they believed that He would help, Jesus said to the sick man, 'Son, your sins are forgiven!'"

Don't give up when you encounter a barrier that impedes your progress to attain a goal. Pray for God's wisdom to see your ultimate goal that brings honor and praise to our mighty God, i.e., remember *Faith and Trust*. God's plan for your life will then unfold before you.

Below is a quote from the Tupperware magazine, *TODAY*. It is an example of Cindy's creative thinking. Excellent results were realized, so much so that the Tupperware organization recognized her efforts in *Tupperware Regional* magazine.

"Tupperware Goes Down on the Farm"
Here's a real Tupperware "first," a party on the farm, literally.
Hostesses Diane and Winnie Shaffer wanted to have an outdoor party
On their farmland just outside Sunbury, Pennsylvania. Cindy Reitz,
Manager of "The Faith and Trust" unit at Dodson enterprises, was
happy to oblige. Guests sat on milk cans and watched Cindy
demonstrate from a display set up on haystacks! After the party,
guests and hostesses ushered Cindy into the barn where she learned
to hand milk a cow . . . "very, slowly," Cindy cautioned. Oh, by the
way, refreshments were tumblers of fresh milk . . . what else?

CHALLENGE:

When was the last time you did some creative thinking and decision making? If you intend to bring honor and glory to God and not to yourself, God will honor your efforts and thus truly bless you. Let me challenge you to keep a written log of decisions that you make for one week. Then at the end of the week, review the decisions:

- How many were very safe?
- How many were aggressive?
- How many were way outside the box?
- Did you trust God to be more aggressive?
- Were you playing it safe 90% of the time?

7
Listen to Those Close to You

Regarding my employment with the City of Sunbury (Chapter 5), I turned in my resignation letter to Mayor Morgan on September 11, 1979. According to my contract, I was required to work until November 11th. If I did not have a job to go to at that time (November 11th), I would not be eligible for unemployment compensation because I voluntarily resigned. This made me nervous, as I considered our family budget: mortgage, groceries for five, car expenses, contributions to our church, etc.

I immediately began my search for employment. I networked with my fellow human resource professionals, the United States Employment Agency, as well as family members and friends. I invested many hours in this search and wasn't even offered a human resource entry-level position.

Then in October 1979, following a very unsuccessful day pounding the pavement, I parked the car in the basement and began to talk to God disrespectfully. Later that same day, I did talk to God again. This time, I sought His forgiveness for the negative attitude I demonstrated earlier.

Upon entering the kitchen, I found Cindy working on supper. I looked very depressed and tired, based on her comments to me regarding my appearance. She immediately tried to lift my spirits. However, she met a "brick wall" and had little success. Silence permeated the room!

After what seemed like many minutes, the silence was interrupted with the sound of a telephone ringing. Cindy looked at me and said, "Answer the phone, Ron, there is your next job." I gave Cindy a very suspicious look and said, "Are you trying to be funny?" I answered the telephone, and it was Mr. Roy Goodlander, Personnel Manager at H. Warshow and Sons, Inc., located in Milton, Pennsylvania.

The telephone conversation was relatively short. Mr. Goodlander indicated that he wanted to talk with me regarding a position at H. Warshow and Sons, Inc. We established a day and location to meet, exchanged pleasantries, and ended the telephone conversation. I turned around and gave Cindy a very suspicious and cautious look.

Cindy asked, "Who was on the telephone?" I indicated that I was sure she was just playing with me; she knew who was on the telephone because they probably called earlier while I was out looking for a job. Cindy began to make gestures and short comments that were intended to convince me that she had no idea who had just called. I became silent, thinking that for some reason, Cindy was trying to give me a difficult time.

Finally, I broke the silence by saying, "When the telephone rang you said, 'Answer the telephone Ron, there is your next job.'" Cindy did not seem to know what to say next, so she just stared at me. This was one of the few times in our fifteen-plus years of marriage that she was at a loss for words!

After several additional comments of this nature, I indicated that the gentleman on the telephone was Mr. Roy Goodlander, Personnel Manager at H. Warshow and Sons, and he wanted to talk with me regarding an opening they will soon have at their Milton plant.

After meeting with Mr. Goodlander and soon after that meeting with the Vice President of Operations, Norman Schneider, I was offered the position of Personnel Manager for H. Warshow and Sons Inc., effective January 1, 1980. Also, note that Mr. Goodlander would continue to work, in a training capacity, until his scheduled date for retirement, July 1, 1980.

Upon reflection of this day's events, the following questions surfaced in my mind:

- Why did I make comments that sounded like I was giving up on God?

- Why did Cindy say, "Answer the telephone Ron, there is your next job?

- Why did I not believe Cindy?

GOD PROVIDED WISDOM

As a Christian couple, we were praying that God would answer our prayers and do it in His timing. In our case, God was very clear; so clear that we believed it couldn't be true! Remember, we are asking Him to answer our prayers in His timing, which can be NOW!

Bottom Line: Don't assume that the answers to your prayers have to be way out in the future for them to be true! Also, often we feel that the answers to our prayers can't be as obvious as it was in this case. God does not always try to develop the virtue of patience with every request we make!

Remember James 1:5–9 (TLB), "If you want to know what God wants you to do, ask Him, and He will gladly tell you, for He is always ready to give a bountiful supply of wisdom to all who ask Him; He will not resent it. But when you ask Him, be sure that you really expect Him to tell you, for a doubtful mind will be as unsettled as a wave of the sea that is driven and tossed by the wind; and every decision you then make will be uncertain, as you turn first this way and then that. If you don't ask with faith, don't expect the Lord to give you any solid answer. A Christian who doesn't amount to much in this world should be glad, for he is great in the Lord's sight."

CHALLENGE:
Write three significant decisions that you were faced with during the past week. Were any of your prayers answered yet? Write down how you are addressing and dealing with the message from James 1:6 (TLB) "But when you ask Him, be sure that you really expect Him to tell you, for a doubtful mind will be as unsettled as a wave of the sea that is driven and tossed by the wind."

8
The ABCs of Amazing GRACE

Two thousand years after the death of Jesus Christ, the idea that God can love and accept a sinner is such amazingly good news. Some of us still do not know how to deal with it effectively. Also, unresolved sinful actions from the past will impede our ability to rise above life challenges that surface in the future. Yes, it is difficult to accept that God loves all sinners. However, this is clearly the message of the Bible.

As in an example from the Old Testament, the people of Israel were never the people God meant them to be. God continually rebuked them and punished them, but they remained His people. They murmured against Moses in the wilderness, even after God delivered them from their enslavement in Egypt. Still, when they thirsted for water, God provided water by telling Moses to smite the rock.

In the New Testament, Paul records in Romans 5:6-8 (TLB), "When we were utterly helpless, with no way of escape, Christ came at just the right time and died for us sinners who had no use for Him. Even if we were good, we really wouldn't expect anyone to die for us, though, of course, that might be barely possible. But God showed his great love for us by sending Christ to die for us while we were still sinners." The implications of such doctrine are mind-boggling—certainly Amazing Grace!

Now, as a result of this doctrine, we must realize that we can live our lives openly and freely because God accepts us just as we are. I heard about a young lady who was dancing with a young man when he began kissing her, and she hesitated and said, "You want to kiss me out here in front of

God and everybody?" There are times when I feel like I am hiding some things from God. A classic example is when someone harms me, and I have a desire to get even.

Grace does not mean that God turns His head when we do wrong. Nothing is hidden from Him. He loves us, accepts us, and has provided the shed blood of His Son on the cross to pay the price of our sin. He will forgive us. If we take the letters that make up the word "grace" and use them as the first letter for the following words, "God's Riches At Christ's Expense," we have a statement that very clearly describes God's intentions for us. We must realize this statement, in no way, indicates we need to be worthy of salvation, or we need to earn salvation, but rather it is something given to us freely through Christ's sacrificial death on the cross.

We have made mistakes in our lives, perhaps committed terrible sins. And we have allowed those mistakes to become a wall between God and us. These sins are not a wall that God has erected, but one we have erected. There is no wall that God will not cross; this, my friends, is what GRACE is all about. Our sin is not the problem. It is our refusal to accept God's forgiveness and love! We must remember because of God's Riches At Christ's Expense, God forgives all our sins, past present and future!

If only we could continuously hear Jesus say, "You are accepted, you belong, and you are my child. Relax and let God love you, you do not have to prove your worth, you have been bought with a price, remember God's Riches At Christ's Expense!" And then, if we can show His love within our family, we will have a family focused on love.

Finally, there is another thing that God's Amazing Grace can do for us; it can enable us to be a happier person. At some point in time, guilt sets in when we reflect on our wrong actions. The world tells us to go after happiness for ourselves, even at the expense of others. God tells us to seek God's forgiveness through God's Grace. This will then fill us with a desire to love and serve all people, resulting in happiness.

We can live happily in the knowledge that God loves us. We can truly love others. We can genuinely accept others, forgive them, and have compassion for them. It is a gift, not something that we earn, but a gift God freely offers to each of us.

GOD PROVIDED WISDOM

On earth, happiness is found in the pursuit of happiness for the *self*; however, happiness, according to God, is found in the pursuit of Christian love and service to *others*.

Matthew 5:7 (TLB): "Happy are the kind and merciful, for they shall be shown mercy."

True happiness results in being *merciful*: forgiving, compassionate, gracious, forbearing, and humane.

Happiness throughout all eternity is as simple as "God's ABCs of GRACE"

CHALLENGE:

Will you accept God's love, His forgiveness, His pardon, His amazing GRACE? What past sinful actions do you need to address through God's GRACE? Once you have identified those you harmed, will you seek their forgiveness?

If you do these things, you will be happier, and you will be demonstrating God's love!

9
West Chester University Football

Athletics were always a big part of my life. Early in my marriage, I became very interested in football officiating. In the early 1980s, I was deeply involved in high school, Division II college, and Division III college football officiating. A significant time commitment on my part was required. Thus, having an understanding wife was critical.

These were some of the best days of our lives as a family. For example, Cindy, and our youngest son Adam, occasionally went with me to college games. Adam loved to wear his red football uniform and run around on the football field after the game.

One very memorable experience of how our Lord used football officiating to impact our family, took place at a Division II game at West Chester University. It was game time, so Cindy and Adam made their way to the bleachers. Cindy, as usual, began to interact with the people seated around her. Through this conversation, Cindy learned that one of the female college students seated beside her was dating the star running back for West Chester. Also, Cindy found out that her boyfriend had dyslexia and had all his college textbooks on audiotapes. This information was of interest to Cindy since Adam was recently diagnosed dyslectic.

When Adam heard this discussion between his mother and the college student, his ears perked up like a rabbit's ears on the first day of small game hunting. Adam demonstrated this interest because we had recently obtained audiotapes of several books for him. His initial reaction was that he would not use them. However, with this information regarding a dyslectic college player, as well as after the game being able to meet him, made a very positive impression on Adam. Thus, in the future, when Adam lacked focus, became lazy, etc., we reminded him of the West Chester player who was able to fulfill his dream to play college football because he accepted the fact that he needed to use the tapes. "You, too, Adam," we said, "can fulfill your dream with hard work and focus just like the dyslectic running back from West Chester." This was another example of how God prepared us for future needs through the example of the West Chester University football player.

GOD PROVIDED WISDOM

If the West Chester football player was a Christian, raised in a Christian home, his parents might have been asking all sorts of "why" questions as to why they had to deal with a dyslectic son. Today, we can look back and say that probably one of the "whats" that God wanted to accomplish through the West Chester player was for him to be a motivating force for Adam.

In addition to the lessons regarding Adam's dyslexia noted above, a valuable life lesson that I learned from football officiating was never to give up and to be creative when you desire something.

For example, I made my first attempt to become a college football official by joining a chapter of the Eastern Association of Intercollegiate Football Officials (EAIFO); the closest chapter was in Philadelphia.

My first attempt failed. When I asked for the reasons I failed, the chapter officers told me, "We don't know you; you live so far away, and we don't have the opportunity to see you work high school games."

Through focused prayer, I decided to see if the Athletic Director at Bucknell University would assist me in obtaining the names and contact information for officials assigned to work Bucknell University home football games. With this information, I could determine if any of the assigned officials are from the Philadelphia EAIFO Chapter, and I would be able to contact the head official and ask for his permission to arrive early and attend his pre-game conference. In each game I was granted permission, along with permission to join the crew at half time and at the end of the game to listen in on their review of the game. As it turned out, I was able to follow this approach for four home games at Bucknell University.

In April 1979, I made my second attempt to become a member of the Philadelphia Chapter. The interview was headed in a similar direction to the previous failed interview attempt. Then I heard Mr. Tom Farr, one of the officials I met at a Bucknell game. Mr. Farr said, "Mr. Reitz went the extra mile and came to games at Bucknell University to participate in our pre-game conference meetings. He did this as a learning experience and an opportunity to get to know members of our chapter. I think he should be given favorable action on his application." With this support from a long-term member of the chapter like Mr. Farr, I knew right away that I was in!

CHALLENGE:

Do you love sports? Do you participate in sports without the involvement of immediate family members? Have your spouse and children asked you to stay home with them?

- Read **Hebrews 12:1-6** (TLB).

- Write two examples of sports where you have been involved by yourself. Document your plan to get family members involved. Tell them you are doing this and give them a date when this plan will be made available. Put up a calendar and cross off days to build expectations.

- Do you have a son or daughter who would like to meet a sports icon that seems virtually impossible to meet? I challenge you to write a letter to _____ from the _____ team. "cc" the letter to the team's front office and I bet you will receive a response! You won't know until you try.

10
Cindy Suggests a Future Spouse!

We were closing in on the end of another year, 1984. Cindy was reviewing the early November Tupperware sales produced by her unit, *Faith and Trust*. During this time, I was reading the *Sunbury Daily Item* newspaper and the kids were in bed.

Our living room was tranquil; one could easily hear even a tiny pin drop. The silence was broken by Cindy saying to me, "Ron, if anything ever happens to me, you know the secretary down at the district ABC office?" I hesitated and said, "Yes, I know who you mean." Cindy proceeded, "I think she would make a good mother for our kids and a good wife for you."

Now, how does a husband respond to a comment like that? (I know, very carefully!) I paused and then threw up a quick prayer asking God for a hefty dose of wisdom. Then slowly, I said, "Honey, that is good to know; however, you and I are both very healthy, and I think God has plans for us as a family for a long time into the future." Cindy and I remained seated and stared at each other as if to say, "What just happened?"

Approximately two weeks later, I had a horrifying dialogue with a Pennsylvania state trooper. He said, "I'm sorry, Mr. Reitz, but your wife was dead on arrival at the Williamsport Hospital earlier today."

GOD PROVIDED WISDOM

Was God preparing me for Cindy's car accident and how He would use her death to remind me that Jesus conquered the grave? Was God reminding me we need to tell others of His promise to return one day? That we need to accept Jesus as our Savior now to be prepared for death or Christ's return, whichever comes first?

It became clear to me that this was a "What" that God wanted to be accomplished as a result of this tragedy. God provided me with many opportunities to share the gospel to many people, i.e., supply/cover for pastors who are on vacation; three-year appointment as a Certified Lay Leader in the United Church of Christ denomination; six-year appointment as a Certified Lay Minister in the United Methodist Church denomination.

One day I will be in heaven looking forward to seeing how many people come up to me and say, "I am here in heaven because you shared the gospel with me." And, I will respond, "Praise the Lord."

CHALLENGE:

How many people can you reach for Christ? Keep in mind that you may have significant time on earth to do so, or like Cindy, the time may be quite short. Remember, a person's eternal status is at stake. Let me challenge you to get busy!

11
Responding to Untimely Deaths

Late Wednesday afternoon, December 5, 1984, I was in my office at H. Warshow & Sons, Inc., Milton, Pennsylvania. I had spent the past several hours trying to locate my wife, Cindy.

The day before, Cindy, along with her mother Margret Shumaker, was scheduled to pick up her father, Harry, at the Williamsport Hospital. He was in the hospital for a surgical procedure and was scheduled to go home. However, when Cindy and Margret arrived at the hospital, Harry's blood pressure was elevated, and so it was recommended he stay in the hospital one more day. They returned home without him and made plans to go back for him the next day.

It was now early evening on December 5th, and Cindy and Margret had not arrived at the hospital. Earlier in the afternoon, I spoke to Cindy's younger sister, Pat. She confirmed through hospital personnel that no one had come to pick up Harry.

I finally contacted a Pennsylvania state trooper, who was willing to provide me with some facts. He told me that my wife Cindy was dead on arrival at the Williamsport Hospital earlier that afternoon.

With this news, feelings and emotions hit me like a brick wall. I began to pray. "I need strength, I need wisdom. Help me, Lord, to maintain my faith and trust in you."

It was getting late and my parents, who lived in Sunbury, were watching the children that evening after school. I called my mother to confirm that they were still at their house. Having confirmed their status, I drove to Sunbury.

While driving, my thoughts turned to my children: Adam was nine years old and very interested in sports; Heather was eleven years old and very interested in the piano and her dolls; Bryan was fourteen years old and was a creative interior decorator, who loved to arrange flowers and stencil furniture and walls.

Upon arriving at my parents' home, I asked everyone to take a seat in the family room. I broke the silence in the room when I said, "Your mother and grandma went home to be with Jesus this afternoon. They were both killed in an accident."

I hardly had the words out of my mouth when pure bedlam erupted. My kids began screaming, yelling, crying, jumping on furniture, making horrible faces, etc. Then came the "Why" questions:

- Why did this happen?
- Why did mommy have to pick up grandpa?
- Why didn't grandpa come home yesterday when he was supposed to?
- Why was grandpa's blood pressure too high yesterday?
- Why wasn't Mommy going slower so she would have passed in front of the truck?
- Why Mommy? She was such a kind Christian.
- Why didn't God take a bad person?
- Mommy was always helping others; why did God take her?

My responses to the kids focused on the concept, "You can live to be 100, and you will not receive any answers that will totally satisfy you. You will suffer greatly because no reasonable answers will be found. Bottom line—no reasonable answer(s) exist for most "why" questions. However, you can control how you respond by "what" you do and say."

Then one of the children said, "What are we going to do now?"

I responded to this last question by saying, "We are going to pray, and we are going to look for ways to support and trust God in doing what He wants to accomplish through all of this." Then I began to pray, "Dear God, we need your help! We don't understand why mommy and grandma had to die now. Please help us and give us the ability to make good decisions and to assist you in all that you want to accomplish through these events. Amen!"

GOD PROVIDED WISDOM

Foundation for Prayer Activity:
Perfect Words: Psalm 119:96-97
Make me Wise: Psalm 119:98-100
Remain Obedient: Psalm 119:101-103
Your Word Lights My Path:
    Psalm 119:104-105
See also Ephesians 1:15-21

Key Points regarding prayer:
Pray—Wait (when time permits)—Act
Request Blessings for Others
Pray in a quiet location (Listen)
Rest in God (Try hard to not WORRY about anything)
Sincere prayer will change our heart and bring us closer to God

Note: It wasn't long until God involved our family members in accomplishing some of what He wanted to accomplish through all of this: Bryan and Heather had a friend who experienced the death of her mother due to a heart attack. As soon as Bryan and Heather heard this news they came running to me and said, "Dad, please take us to see Carolyn right away because her mom just died and we know how she feels" Praise God, Bryan and Heather were putting their focus on a "what" question!

CHALLENGE:

In the upcoming week, prayerfully consider three people who need your attention, i.e., kind words through a telephone call, kind words on a written note, and a helpful hand with tasks around the house. Once God has revealed these people to you, follow through and make the call, write the note, and do the task. Result: your focus will start to shift to others and what you can do for them.

12
It is OK to Throw Stones

Fortunately, we were at my parents' home when I told my children that their mommy and grandma were promoted to heaven because my parents always had a calming influence on my children.

Bryan, our oldest son, stated that he needed to go for a walk. The evening had set in, and the air was cool, and the neighborhood houses were decorated with Christmas lights. With Bryan's permission, I got my jacket and walked along with him.

As soon as we left the house, the "why" questions began again. Although I couldn't answer his "why" questions, I sensed it was good for him to express them.

I felt so positive about this time walking with Bryan that when we returned to my parents' home, I asked Heather if she wanted to go for a walk. She said yes! She, too, asked many "why" questions.

Upon returning with Heather from our walk, I asked Adam if he wanted to go for a walk. Little did I know that this walk with Adam would set the stage and direction for many of my future decisions and actions.

After walking and talking with Adam for about ten minutes, he stopped in his tracks and said, "I want to do something for mommy right now." I was somewhat taken aback with a statement of this nature coming from a nine-year-old! I asked him what he wanted to do for mommy.

ADAM: "I want to throw a stone."
DAD: "You want to throw a stone?"

ADAM: "Yes, dad, I want to throw a stone for mommy!"

DAD: "OK, let's think about this now" (I am pausing as much as I can so I can pray for wisdom in this teaching moment).

DAD: "We need to consider several things, such as finding a stone in the dark."

ADAM: "I found one, dad."

DAD: "We need to make sure you throw the stone in a direction, so no one is hurt."

ADAM: "Over in this direction is an empty lot."

DAD: "Keep in mind that your arm is not loosened; don't hurt your arm."

ADAM: "OK."

What happened next was priceless. Adam began to swing his arm and shoulder back and forth slowly. He then gradually swung his arm faster. Adam then began to swing his arm in a full circle while holding onto the stone.

Adam said, "Dad, we found a stone; I loosened up my arm and shoulder; over in this direction is an empty lot."

I then said to Adam, "It looks like you are ready to go!"

Adam stared out over the lot. Finally, with tears rolling down my cheeks, and after what seemed like an eternity, Adam began moving his arm, and with one smooth motion, he threw the stone out into the night time air. With great confidence and authority, while looking up into the dark, dismal sky, he said, "There mommy, that one is for you!"

Adam then turned to me and said, "Dad, we can now go back to grandma and grandpa's house. I'm finished!" Adam was always a very active child. He was happiest when he could be doing something physical. Throughout his life, physical activity was what he turned to when he had excess energy; also, he used weightlifting and football to express his emotions and feelings.

GOD PROVIDED WISDOM

God created our bodies in such a fashion that enables us to accomplish much in the arena of physical work. However, it is also essential to be "energy" filled for spiritual matters. Paul's letter to Timothy (1 Timothy 4:7-8) tells us not to waste time arguing over foolish ideas and silly myths and legends. We are encouraged to spend our time in the exercise of keeping spiritually in shape. Our bodies are the "temple" of the Lord, and thus we are directed to be physically active. This includes being active in ways that will keep us "fit" and able to get energy out of our bodies to do needed tasks. However, never cease from obtaining spiritual energy to use in battling the devil and his evil demons.

CHALLENGE:
Read the New Testament book of 1 Timothy. Consider prayerfully the concepts presented that relate directly to you. For example, does 1 Timothy 5:3 (TLB) apply? i.e., "The church should take loving care of women whose husbands have died if they don't have anyone else to help them."

13
The Telephone Call that Started It All

In the fall of 1982, I became active in the Certified Lay Minister program of the United Church of Christ (UCC). My geographic area of service was to UCC churches in central Pennsylvania.

From October 1982 to June 1983, I provided Sunday morning service support to the Line Mountain Charge. The Charge was comprised of two churches: Salem UCC in Schuylkill County, Pennsylvania, and Christ's UCC in Northumberland County, Pennsylvania.

Simultaneous with the Line Mountain Charge being successful in calling a permanent pastor, Grace United Church of Christ in Troxelville, Pennsylvania, needed a half-time pastor to cover the ministerial needs of their congregation. Grace UCC offered their half-time position to me effective January 1, 1984.

As I was settling into my new roles, I witnessed God doing great things as a result of our ministry efforts founded upon planting seeds focused on God's love and care provided through His Son, Jesus.

In September 1984, I became aware of an event sponsored by the Fellowship of Christian Athletes, titled *Athletes Speak Out*. The Valley Forge Music Fair, an entertainment venue located in Devon, Pennsylvania, outside of Philadelphia, was hosting the annual event. The facility was constructed in a theater in the round style, seating approximately 3,000 guests.

This concept became a means to present top performers and productions of popular musicals at reasonable prices outside of the big cities.

The *Athletes Speak Out* annual event for 1984 was being held on Monday evening, December 3rd. The Grace UCC administrative board approved the renting of a coach bus to attend this athlete-focused event. Several well-known professional athletes would be there to share their testimonies, a real drawing card in our efforts to spread the Gospel of Jesus Christ!

One of the presenters, and also the Master of Ceremonies for the evening, was Pat Williams, the General Manager and Vice-President of the Philadelphia 76ers of the National Basketball Association. The program indicated that Pat was very active in the ministry efforts of The Fellowship of Christian Athletes. It was clear from his stories, jokes, and comments that he was also very active in his daily walk with Jesus.

Pat Williams's authentic faith was clearly demonstrated in the following scenario. The *Athletes Speak Out* event that we attended was on Monday. Two days later, Wednesday, December 5th, my wife Cindy and her mother, Margaret Shumaker, were killed instantly in a head-on crash with a tractor-trailer truck on Route 15, south of Williamsport, Pennsylvania. A close friend of mine, Mark Bittner, had gone along on the bus to this event. When Mark heard of my wife's tragic death, he was speechless. Mark could not believe what he was hearing and immediately went into prayer mode.

After a short time, Mark began to focus on the question, "What" can I do to help my friend Ron and his family? Mark's thoughts then turned to the *Athletes Speak Out* event and, in particular, Pat Williams. Mark decided to try and call Pat Williams and request prayer.

Mark obtained Pat William's telephone number, and a secretary answered. When Mark said, "This is Mark Bittner, may I speak to Mr. Williams?" Mark was amazed that she put him right through to Mr. Williams. Also, Mark was surprised that Mr. Williams accepted the call.

In essence, Mark said, "A good friend of mine was with me at the *Athletes Speak Out* event in Valley Forge earlier this week. We were both very impressed with your Christian witness, and I want to ask you to pray for my friend because yesterday, his wife was killed in an accident." Pat

Williams said to Mark, "I will pray for your friend. What are his name and address? I want to write to him, send him a book, and send him tickets to an upcoming 76ers basketball game." And, that is not the end of the story.

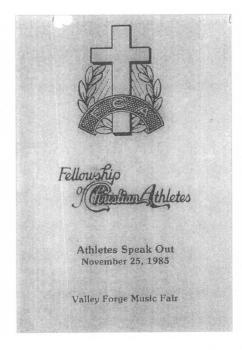

Athletes Speak Out
November 25, 1985

Valley Forge Music Fair

Pat Williams followed through on everything he promised, and when we went to the 76ers game, he met us and showed us around the facility. At my suggestion, he invited us to come to the *Athletes Speak Out* event scheduled for November 25, 1985. He also coordinated with the Fellowship of Christian Athletes organization the agenda item of sharing my testimony and the events surrounding my wife's and mother-in-law's tragic accident. WOW! Clearly, I viewed this series of events as "whats" that God wanted to be accomplished from this tragedy and all the "why" questions surrounding it.

At the following year's *Athletes Speak Out* event, before the program, I was invited backstage for a meet and greet session with the professional athletes who would make presentations at the main event. Question: "Did you ever shake hands with Reggie White, defensive end for the Philadelphia Eagles? When I did, his hands and forearms were so large that he swallowed my hand up to my armpit!"

And then, what a neat opportunity this was to share God's love to several thousand people. This all started with a simple telephone call from my friend, Mark Bittner, to Pat Williams. These events were possible because Mark Bittner and Pat Williams were focused on "What," not "Why!" They were looking for ways to have positive things come out of negative events.

IN MEMORY OF..........

CINDY REITZ

Ron and Cindy Reitz and children Bryan, Heather and Adam attended the 1984 Athletes Speak Out. This was their last night together as a family. On December 5th the Lord sent His "death angel" down to earth to take Cindy and her mother onto their eternal home in Heaven.

Cindy loved the Lord and her life as a wife, mother, daughter, businesswoman and involved church member witnessed to this daily.

Cindy was dearly loved by her family and many f .ends. Her passing leaves a void in many people's live' and activities. However, as Ron as told us, it wa. Cindy's wish that people not mourn her death but rejoice in the fact that she was at peace in Eternity.

The Fellowship of Christian Athletes join the Reitz family in praising the Lord for His gift to us in the life of Cindy and for His love that she so beautifully expressed.

GOD PROVIDED WISDOM

When Dealing With "Scolding Hot Water" Issues in Life
Death of mother and grandmother

Consider Psalm 91: 1-2 (TLB):

"We live within the shadow of the Almighty, sheltered by the God who is above all gods. This I declare, that He alone is my refuge, my place of safety; He is my God, and I am trusting Him."

- **Confirm your Faith:** John 20:30-31 (TLB): "Jesus's disciples saw Him do many other miracles besides the ones told about in this book, but these are recorded (miracles) so that you will believe that He is the Messiah, the Son of God, and that believing in Him you will have life."

- **Read/Search Scriptures:** I Timothy 4:13-16 (TLB): "Until I get there, read and explain the Scriptures to the church; preach God's Word."

- **Worship regularly:** Matthew 4:8-10 (TLB): "The Scriptures say, worship only the Lord God. Obey only Him."

- **Remember Promise:** Philippians 4:13 (KJV): "I can do all things through Christ who strengthen me." and John 14:15-16 (TLB) "If you love me, obey me; and I will ask the Father and He will give you another Comforter, and He will never leave you."

CHALLENGE:

Select from your circle of friends, co-workers, neighbors, fellow club members, etc., one who is struggling with a very challenging issue. For two weeks, use the above-suggested Scriptures daily (find a quiet location without interruptions), and respond as you are directed from the Holy Spirit. You will be amazed by the results!

14
Three Different Ways to Respond

From my observations, Bryan, Heather, and Adam each responded differently to mommy and grandma's death.

Adam was always physical and thus expressed himself through actions that were filled with movement, activity, excitement, noise, etc. (Controlled Physical Activity).

Heather focused on becoming more organized and striving to be very helpful to others. She appreciated when people recognized her skills and how proud her mother would be (Developing Organization Skills).

Bryan was skilled in the arts, and thus, he loved to work with his mother in stenciling, painting, and flower arranging (Developing Artistic Skills).

I have outlined below several steps I used to try and support each of them as they expressed themselves and their interests/skills while coping with the death of their mother and grandmother.

Controlled Physical Activity (Adam)

- Help child choose an appropriate activity;

- If you don't have the necessary skill/interest for this activity, communicate this information to an adult who has this same skill/interest;

- Get additional help if needed (i.e., weight training should be done with at least one other person present);

- Consider any dangers and/or unsafe actions and take the needed step(s) to ensure safety;

- Take some time to focus on what and why you are doing this action/activity;

- One such activity that Adam used was weightlifting. We discussed options with the school athletic trainer and found out that he had access to a trainer and free weights at the school.

Developing Organization Skills (Heather)

- Present to the child some examples of situations where good organization skills are demonstrated;

- Be sure to recognize when the child demonstrates organization skills (i.e., make a "big deal" of it but not in front of other people);

- Talk about and help them appreciate how organization skills will be a benefit to them more and more as they grow older and receive more responsibility;

- One such activity that Heather responded to in this manner is "grocery shopping" (see chapter 15).

Developing Controlled Skills (Bryan)

- Select a skill to develop in your child that you know the deceased person possessed. Then communicate to another person, who has this skill, what you plan to do (i.e., paint a picture of your deceased relative/friend, etc.);

- Get help if needed; i.e., the child wants to erect a statue on the roof of a building. In this case, you will need to consider any dangers and/or unsafe actions;

- Move forward showing both excitement and confidence;

- Bryan loved activities with his mother involving flowers and stenciling. They often worked together on projects around the home. Several months following Cindy's death, Bryan surprised me by stenciling a pattern above the chair rail in the newly remolded living room. Also, during this same time frame, he stenciled a pattern at ceiling height in my bedroom. This was a big move for Bryan. I sensed that he had his mother at his side (so to speak), and he was much more relaxed and content.

GOD PROVIDED WISDOM

Following other people in their efforts to respond effectively to tragedies, Paul writes in his letter to the Ephesians the importance of following Christ in all that we do: Ephesians 5:2 (TLB). "Be full of love for others, following the example of Christ who loved you and gave himself to God as a sacrifice to take away your sins. And God was pleased, for Christ's love for you was like sweet perfume to him."

CHALLENGE:
For this and the next chapter, if you have children or grandchildren in the age range of five to eighteen, who have lost a significant person due to death, compare their interests and skills to those summarized in these two chapters. You never know when you will be in a position to use this approach to assist a friend or relative in assisting their child with this challenging adjustment.

15
I Love to Grocery Shop

Heather is my only daughter. I was also blessed with six sons, Bryan, Adam, Justin, Landon, Kaleb, and Marcus. I remarried following Cindy's death. Being my only daughter, Heather has always held a very special place in my heart! She has always been a very thoughtful and kind person. To this day, she continues to be very loving and is always looking for ways to help others and to assist the disadvantaged person.

I thought it would be helpful to expand on some of the additional elements of Heather's daily activities that were helpful to me. Part of the reason that I am aware of these activities is that Heather was willing to express herself and ask questions. Unfortunately, from my experience, young people often "clam up" in times of tragedy, such as the death of a parent.

Several individuals assisted Heather through this tough time: Aunt Pat (Cindy's younger sister) and Grandma Reitz (my mother) were two such persons. Making cookies, cleaning the house, cooking, baking, grocery shopping are just a few of the activities noted. It was evident to me that by doing these activities/chores, she would be making mom proud of her. Also, these activities kept her busy and her mind off of being sad.

During this time of adjustment, I had the foresight to see the value in these activities for Heather. I recall that I used to let her go grocery shopping while I went next door to work out at the YMCA. And if you ask Heather about this topic today, she will tell you that she felt like she was helpful to me, and she was! Also, even today, as a dedicated wife and mother of many years, she still says, "I LOVE TO GROCERY SHOP!"

GOD PROVIDED WISDOM

At a young age, Heather showed excellent judgment and common sense as she responded to the guidance and support from adults who wanted to be helpful. Proverbs 3:13-15 (TLB) says, "The man who knows right from wrong and has good judgment and common sense is happier than the man who is immensely rich. For such wisdom is far more valuable than precious jewels. Nothing else compares with it." Also, Proverbs 22:6 (TLB) says, "Teach a child to choose the right path, and when he is older, he will remain upon it."

Use good judgment and common sense in helping young people through many of the difficult adjustments needed when challenging events such as the death of a parent is involved. A simple task such as grocery shopping can be a big help to you and the child/teenager.

CHALLENGE:
(See the last page of chapter 14.)

16
Allow Others to Serve You

A huge mistake I made immediately following Cindy's death was not encouraging others to serve me. I totally overlooked Matthew 20:28 (TLB), which says, "Your attitude must be like my own, for, I the Messiah, did not come to be served, but to serve, and to give my life as a ransom for many." Since I was not allowing others to serve me, I denied others the ability to follow Christ's example! Instead, I developed an attitude that I would be able to persevere and effectively handle the many dynamics that would come my way.

The reality was that overnight I became a widower with three children that needed lots of attention. I thought the way I should react to all of this was to be independent and handle all our needs by myself.

One of the initial indicators of my mistake in judgment was brought to my attention by Dr. Horace Sills, President of Penn Central Conference of the United Church of Christ. His letter came to me a few weeks following Cindy's death. Dr. Sills was part of the ministerial support I had during those very challenging days following Cindy's accident. Specifically, Dr. Sills said, "Allow others to support your family during these challenging times. And, let the people minister to you as well."

Since that letter, I have learned a great deal about being a servant, even how to be a joyful servant. Under the GOD PROVIDES WISDOM section of this chapter is a handout that I have used in attempting to get this servanthood concept communicated to others! It is a powerful concept of the Christian faith that enables us to make disciples for Jesus Christ.

So, when my son Adam was promoted to heaven, I was again faced with a very long list of tasks that needed to be accomplished promptly. I was determined to get my ego out of the way and allow others to serve my family and me.

From a practical standpoint, what worked well for me was a spreadsheet. I developed a system where on the left column was listed the things that needed to be done. The next column listed a due date or a reasonable completion date. This system accomplished several things for me:

- it indicated to the person who was offering help that I was taking their offer very seriously;

- it provided an administrative process to keep track of recurring responsibilities (i.e., car inspection, yard work, caring for pets or farm animals, keeping in touch with teachers, etc.);

- it provided a system to follow up on progress being made with the assignment;

- it enabled me to see how excited and happy people were that they were given something to do that was not just "busy" work but very real tasks and projects.

On a side note, when you are the potential "servant giver" in a situation where a close family member died (i.e., the mother of your neighbor; the child of a co-worker, etc.) call a few days before the funeral and tell the neighbor, co-worker, etc. that you are bringing breakfast to their home on the day of the funeral. Ask them approximately how many persons expect to be there, time details, etc. A suggested menu might consist of a Sausage and Peppers Brunch Bake Casserole, a bowl of fruit, small cookies or donut holes, and a container of orange juice. Be assured that the family will resist this offer, but don't let them say no. Remind them that Jesus has called us to be servants, and by not accepting this offer, they will deny you the opportunity to do what our Savior taught. From my experience, long after this event, they will comment on how much they appreciated your efforts, and you can simply reply, "Praise God."

GOD PROVIDED WISDOM

LOVE GOD & LOVE ALL PEOPLE
A RECIPE TO LOVE BY

Blend 1 cup of love and ½ cup kindness; add alternately in small portions, 1 cup appreciation and 3 cups pleasant companionship into which has been sifted 3 tsp deserving praise. Flavor with 1 tsp carefully chosen advice. Lightly fold in 1 cup cheerfulness to which has been added a pinch of sorrow. Pour with tender care into hearts of others and let bake until well matured. Turn out on surface of society; humbly invoke God's blessing, and it will serve all mankind.

Remember, God has given each of us spiritual gifts, talents, and skills to use in assisting others. Romans 12:6-8 (TLB) says, "God has given each of us the ability to do certain things well. So if God has given you the ability to prophesy, then prophesy whenever you can—as often as your faith is strong enough to receive a message from God. If your gift is that of serving others, serve them well. If you are a teacher, do a good job of teaching. If you are a preacher, see to it that your sermons are strong and helpful. If God has given you money, be generous in helping others with it. If God has given you administrative ability and put you in charge of the work of others, take the responsibility seriously. Those who offer comfort to the sorrowing should do so with Christian cheer."

Therefore, if you do not allow others to help you, then you will keep them from using their spiritual gifts as directed by God.

CHALLENGE:
Next time someone offers to do a task for you, only say, "That would be nice," and let them do it. If they have a close family member promoted to heaven, present them with the breakfast offer summarized above.

17
Pat Comes into my Life

Several weeks passed after Cindy's promotion to heaven when her comments regarding a replacement spouse came to mind. The woman mentioned by Cindy was a Secretary for ABC Company.

Over the next several months, I prayed very earnestly regarding Cindy's suggestions. This was an emotional issue for me. Cindy and I had a fantastic relationship (we were married fifteen-plus years), and I truly felt that marriage was the best institution that God had created and ordained. Therefore, I did not want to remain single. However, was the woman Cindy identified right for the kids and me? I also put myself in the presence of this young lady every chance that I had. This was not difficult to do because I had follow-up issues in the greater Sunbury area that occasionally surfaced as a result of Cindy's death. I also continued to minister to the folks at Grace UCC in Troxelville. On at least one occasion, I invited this young lady to travel along with the kids and me at a church sponsored event. However, as I noted to others who asked me about the potential for this relationship to develop, "no rockets" ever shot off in my mind. She was a beautiful person and a friend, but not a future wife for me and stepmother for my three children.

The folks in the Grace UCC congregation were incredibly supportive of my ministry efforts following Cindy's death. On one occasion in March 1985, Floyd and Lucille Mattern were visiting at my home in Sunbury. Their daughter Patricia was a student at the Reading School of Nursing.

Pat was returning to her home in McClure, Pennsylvania, for the weekend. Hearing that her parents were at my home, Pat decided to stop in and visit.

Our time of interaction on that Friday evening made a very positive impression upon me. Many sleepless nights, positive thoughts, and dreams followed. Pat was at the center of all this excitement. The major roadblock that stopped me from moving forward in a relationship with Pat was our age difference, i.e., seventeen years. Also, many people had no problem coming right out and saying that I was moving too fast.

One evening I decided to bring up the subject of dating with my three children. I asked my children how they felt about their dad dating. Bryan (age 15) said he thought it would be OK, but he would not want to double-date with me. Heather (age 13) said she wasn't sure how she felt but thought it would be OK. Adam (age10) asked, "Who would you date?"

I said, "I am considering asking Pat Mattern out on a date."

Adam said, "Dad, how old are you?"

I said, "37."

He then said, "How old is Pat Mattern?"

I said, "Almost 20."

Adam thought for a few moments and said, "You are 37, and Pat is almost 20, WOW! That's a difference of 17 years!"

I then said, "WOW Adam, your math is excellent." Adam then gave me one of those big Adam smiles that, in later years, were synonymous with the name Adam Reitz! I took his smile response as an "OK" for me to date.

An entire book could be written on how the relationship between Pat and I evolved. However, on a Sunday in September 1985, I proposed marriage to Pat. The location for this super emotional event was the large stone outdoor altar, Pisgah Altar, Beaver Springs, PA.

At this time, I was still the Lay Minister at Grace United Church of Christ, Troxelville, Pennsylvania. On this particular Sunday morning, I conducted the morning service as usual. My mother and dad, Pat's parents, Bryan, Heather, Adam, Pat, and I went to Jo-Lees Restaurant in Troxelville for lunch. Following lunch, as pre-planned with my parents, Pat and I went away, and my parents took the children home with them. Pat did not know where we were going, and thus many "why" questions began to come my way.

Upon arrival at the Altar, we walked up the steps onto the top level of this magnificent structure. For a few minutes, we simply enjoyed the view. I then took the diamond ring from my little finger and got down on one knee. My words were very simple. "Pat, I love you. Will you marry me?" "What" will be her response?

The response from Pat was a quivering lip, tears in her eyes, a shaking head in a front and back motion, and an audible "yes" from her quivering lips!

"Praise the Lord, here comes the bride" was my response.

Many years later (30+ years), we had a very neat experience that again involved the Pisgah Altar. I was serving as a Certified Lay Minister at Faith United Methodist Church in Fisherville, Halifax, Pennsylvania. I was appointed by the Bishop June Middleton in July 2012 and served Faith UMC until July 2018. This was a classic small church, except this congregation was willing to step out and try new ministries to make disciples for Jesus Christ!

One of those new ministries was Saturday night out for dinner and a concert. The meal was free, and local gospel singing groups presented the concerts. As time went on, the word spread and attendance rose. These were ideal events for senior folks who were widowed.

The Gospel Bond group from Selinsgrove, Pennsylvania, was one such group that provided music for this type of ministry. While preparing the church for the concert, I noticed a CD cover case with a picture of the Gospel Bond members standing on the steps of the Pisgah Altar.

Immediately memories of joy flooded into my mind! Such memories of joy would not have taken place had I not been led by God to propose to Pat at the Altar. Also, the group sang a song, "The Napkin is Still Folded" that became the basis for a sermon that I was able to prepare and present at a future Easter Sun Rise Service. Please note that I believe all these positive events took place as "whats" that God wanted to be accomplished following Cindy's death. However, let me again state very clearly that I am not suggesting that I am happy that Cindy was killed so that one day these divine experiences would take place. I am, however, stating that when life gives you a set of circumstances that cause "why" questions, you can't dwell on the "whys" but trust God and look into the future for "whats" that will glorify and praise our almighty God. It is not for us to question our God on the "whys" but to realize that our mission is to bring honor and glory to God and trust that the "whats" will eventually come. That is "whats" that will glorify God!

GOD PROVIDED WISDOM

The age issue was always somewhat problematic. I decided to face the issue head-on.

My research brought to my attention several interesting facts regarding my great, great grandpa, Peter Reitz. I learned that Peter's first wife died at a young age. He re-married a woman 17 years younger than him and had several additional children (sounds like me).

Also, I learned some interesting facts regarding Pat's parents. For example, her dad, Floyd, became a widower when he was in his mid-30s and already had three children (sounds like me). He married a woman 12 years younger than him, Lucille, and had one child, Pat. Over the years I have noted that since Pat was raised in an environment of half-sisters and brother; having a father who was much older than her mother (12 years); having in essence two blended families; she (Pat) was well prepared for the family dynamics she was entering into by marrying me!

Clearly, I give God credit for bringing these facts to my attention. It made the transition much smoother. Many evenings at home alone, I searched the scriptures for wisdom as Pat and my relationship continued. Praise God for His Word! For example, Paul's letters to the Corinthians: 1 Corinthians 10, 1 Corinthians 13 (the love chapter), 2 Corinthians 4, 2 Corinthians 6, 2 Corinthians 12.

CHALLENGE:

Consider a major decision before you right now: i.e., change jobs, break a relationship, buy a new home, having elective surgery, etc. Over the next several days, spend time reading the scriptures (Bible) seeking answers to questions that you have regarding this decision. Write down these spiritual communication results that take place between you and the Holy Spirit. Then prayerfully consider these spiritual written points as you make your decision.

18
The Wedding

Reverend Fred Rooming, Pat's cousin, performed our wedding ceremony at Grace UCC, Troxelville, Pennsylvania, on December 28, 1985. I was able to surprise Pat by singing "The Lord's Prayer" during the wedding ceremony, and Pat was able to surprise me by wearing a wedding gown with a beautiful hat. Pat knew how much I liked hats.

Pat and I realized how emotional this ceremony would be for our three children (Bryan, age 15; Heather, age 12; and Adam, age 10). Therefore, we encouraged them to take part in the ceremony. After plenty of encouragement, Bryan agreed to be my best man, Heather said she would play the piano ("The Rose"), and Adam agreed to be the candle lighter.

My father made 6' long candle holders from walnut lumber received from Jack Heeter, a family friend. The candleholders were attached to the inside aisle end of each pew. What an awesome sight to see Adam lighting candleholders made by my dad.

One of the most memorable times for me during the ceremony was when Rev Romig shared the following illustration from *LOOK* magazine regarding the definition of "true love."

An elderly couple entered a restaurant at midday to obtain a bite to eat. The elderly couple moved slowly through the dining area to an empty table in the back of the restaurant.

The husband and wife did not bother to look at the menu. When the waitress came for their order, the elderly gentleman indicated that they would like one roll, some butter, and one cup of hot tea.

Pat and Ron, December 28, 1985

When the waitress brought the order to their table, the gentleman placed the hot cup of tea in front of his wife, and he proceeded to tear the roll in two, and butter both halves. The elderly woman proceeded to sip on the tea, while the elderly gentleman began to eat half of the buttered roll.

After about five minutes, the elderly gentleman passed the second half of the buttered roll to his wife, and the elderly woman passed the remaining hot tea to her husband. The elderly gentleman then took out his false teeth, wiped them off with his napkin, handed them to his wife, and she proceeded to place the false teeth into her mouth. The elderly gentleman then sipped the remaining hot tea, and the elderly woman ate the other half of the buttered roll. The magazine article ended by stating, "This is an example of 'truly' true love!"

Two additional highlights of the church events, both outdoors, were a one-horse open sleigh and two large workhorses pulling a hay wagon. Fortunately, open fields were adjacent to the church.

My sister Judy Dunkelberger provided the beautiful old sleigh; however, she did not have an appropriate size horse. Fortunately, the neighbor had two very large field workhorses; too large to pull the sleigh but perfect for pulling a large hay wagon. The air was crisp and clear. It was a moonlit night, and small piles of snow from an earlier in the week snowfall added to the beauty of the surroundings.

More than three decades later, we continue to love and respect each other. The Lord has also blessed us with four sons: Justin, Landon, Kaleb, and Marcus.

This chapter in my life speaks directly to the "Why/What" issue. I have, on occasion, said to my four sons, "If my first wife Cindy had not been killed, you would not be here. The bottom line (as far as our human minds can comprehend) is that God 'allowed' Cindy's life to end in an accident. As a result of this event, other "Whats" have the potential to take place that otherwise would not have been possible! Specifically, a blended family was created that continues to this day. The memory and love of Cindy remain, and we will be reunited with her in heaven one day."

The giant issues/decisions for me at this juncture of my life were the emotions surrounding Pat and my earthly relationship. Today I often look back and think about how God guided us through this maze of emotions. Today there is an acronym found in many Christian churches, "WWJD," that would have helped make these decisions. The way it works is when faced with a decision, put Jesus in your place, and ask the question to yourself? "What Would Jesus Do?" In other words, since Jesus never sinned, as long as the direction you choose is consistent with Jesus's teachings, you can be confident that you are on the correct path!

When making choices, ask the question: "What Would Jesus Do?"

GOD PROVIDED WISDOM

Remember 1 Peter 2:21b-23 (TLB): "Christ, who suffered for you, is your example. Follow in his steps: He never sinned, never told a lie, never answered back when insulted; when he suffered he did not threaten to get even; he left his case in the hands of God who always judges fairly."

Formula:
Recognize "issue(s)" before you;
Say a prayer seeking wisdom; spend time in the Bible;
Based on Bible insights, ask yourself: "What would Jesus do?"
Make your choice;
If "Jesus like" choice made and issue resolved—Praise God!
If "non-Jesus like" choice made—Seek Forgiveness and try again.

CHALLENGE:
Identify two issues before you that require answers. Using WWJD, see if you can make decisions that are "Jesus like" and that eliminate your unrest.

19
Marion Raises Two Boys

Adam was nine years old when his mother and grandmother were killed in a car accident. Fortunately, Adam continued to reveal many appropriate ways to express his feelings and emotions through physical activities.

Adam played baseball at the midget and little league levels in Sunbury. Over the next several years, he added elementary level basketball, midget football, and free weights training to his list of favorite activities. Under the guidance of Mr. George Fury, Adam received an excellent foundation of knowledge in the area of free-weight strength and conditioning.

By the fall of 1990, Adam had demonstrated many skills in football. These demonstrated skills, as well as his size and work ethic in the weight room, resulted in Adam being moved to the varsity level at Shikellamy High School. Adam had such an outstanding sophomore year that *The Daily Item* selected him as the Susquehanna Valley conference first team's right offensive tackle. Adam was riding high. He was tall, dark, handsome, and recognized as one of the best up-and-coming football stars in the area, and he was only fifteen years old.

One of Adam's good friends was a fellow lineman, Isaac Ramer. Isaac had an older sister, Marion, who had a young son, Jordan. Marion was effective in the role of a single mother, and although she did not reside with Jordan's father, they had a positive relationship, and he was helpful to her in raising Jordan. Although Marion struggled as a single parent, she appreciated the opportunity to raise a child.

Adam frequently visited in Isaac's home. Marion and Adam began dating. Several months later, Marion was pregnant. She decided not to tell anyone who the father was. When Adam heard Marion was pregnant, he assumed that someone else was the father since she didn't contact him.

Adam was an accomplished athlete in school, and many of his classmates looked up to him. Marion went on with her life and pregnancy and, in June 1991, delivered a bouncing baby boy. She named him Drew Vincent Tressler (Tressler was the last name of her first child's father. Marion was planning to marry him; however, this marriage never took place.). Life went on for both Marion and Adam (Adam: high school; Marion: single mom raising two young boys). No further direct contact or interaction between Adam and Marion took place for the next thirteen years.

While Drew was still a toddler, Marion met and married Jody Kuhns. Drew developed a close relationship with his stepfather, and before becoming a teenager, Drew was adopted by Jody. This resulted in Drew's last name being changed to Kuhns.

By the time Drew became a teenager, Marion and Jody where divorced. At this time, Drew had potentially three last names: Tressler (name on his birth certificate and Social Security card); Kuhns (name change shown on Snyder County records for a legal name change); Reitz (the last name of his biological father).

The name Drew Vincent Kuhns was well established in many different areas of Drew's life. Being a quality student, both academically and athletically, resulted in his name becoming well known in the Selinsgrove area. It was decided his name, Drew Vincent Kuhns, would continue to be the name that this hard-working, well-liked young man would retain.

Keep in mind that during all this time, Drew did not know who his biological father was. Also, to the best of our knowledge, Adam was not clear as to whether he had a son. We, his immediate family, did not have a clue that we had a grandson.

GOD PROVIDED WISDOM

Proverbs 7:4 (TLB): Love wisdom like a sweetheart; make her a beloved member of your family.

Exodus 20:12 (TLB): Honor your father and mother, that you may have a long, good life in the land the Lord your God will give you.

Deuteronomy 5:16 (TLB): Honor your father and mother (remember, this is a commandment of the Lord your God); if you do so, you shall have a long, prosperous life in the land he is giving you.

Proverbs 1:7–9 (TLB): How does a man become wise? The first step is to trust and reverence the Lord! Only fools refuse to be taught. Listen to your father and mother. What you learn from them will stand you in good stead; it will gain you many honors.

CHALLENGE:
Consider and discuss how the above verses apply to the single mother. Did you have any persons that you could discuss with the verses summarized above?

20
Homecoming Queen

Tragedies and unanswered "why" questions go together like peas in a pod. Likewise, many "what" do you want to accomplish dynamics are available. The "whats" are only limited in number and magnitude by how far and how much effort you want to put forth, which includes "thinking outside the box."

Homecoming Queen Award: In 1985, a fund was established that enables an annual monetary award to be given to the student body elected Homecoming Queen of Shikellamy High School. (Sunbury Area School District and Northumberland Area School District came together in 1965 to form Shikellamy Area School District. Cindy Shumaker was the first Shikellamy High School Homecoming Queen in 1965). The initial award was presented in fall 1985 by my oldest child, Bryan, a freshman at Shikellamy High School at that time.

One of the most unique and emotional Homecoming Queen Award presentations took place in October 2008. The Homecoming Queen winner was to be announced just before the start of the football game. Drew Kuhns, Cindy's grandson, a senior at Selinsgrove High School and a member of the Selinsgrove football team, was scheduled to present the award. Drew received permission from his coach to be dismissed early from the pregame team session so he could present the award to the Shikellamy Queen. Get the picture: (Shikellamy Queen Award; award in memory of Cindy; Cindy's grandson Drew dressed in a Selinsgrove football uniform; Drew standing on the Shikellamy sideline waiting to present the award; Shikellamy and Selinsgrove are arch-rivals in sports).

One very neat added, unplanned aspect of this presentation was that the Selinsgrove football coach had the entire Selinsgrove team come out of the locker room. The team knelt in the end zone in support of Drew during a very emotional award presentation time! Above pictured is Drew, Homecoming Queen Colleen, and her escort.

The announcer presented the following message as the award was being presented: "At this time we would like to introduce to you Drew Kuhns. Drew is the grandson of Shikellamy's first Homecoming Queen, Cindy Shumaker Reitz. The Cindy Shumaker Reitz Homecoming Award will now be presented by Drew. Cindy Shumaker Reitz was the first Homecoming Queen of Shikellamy High School in 1965. As a result of an automobile accident in December 1984, Cindy was promoted to heaven. The Cindy Shumaker Reitz Homecoming Queen Award was established in memory of Cindy beginning in 1985."

It should be noted that Selinsgrove defeated Shikellamy in this 2008 Homecoming game. Drew and his team went on to play in the Pennsylvania State High School tournament.

The picture above was taken following a win in one of the state tournament games. Attending this game with me were Drew's three uncles, Kaleb, Landon, and Justin.

GOD PROVIDED WISDOM

Ephesians 5:15-17 (TLB):

"So be careful how you act; these are difficult days. Don't be fools; be wise: make the most of every opportunity you have for doing good. Don't act thoughtlessly, but try to find out and do whatever the Lord wants you to."

This passage came to mind when I considered what Drew's football coach did in bringing the entire football team out to witness the award presentation and thus support their teammate, Drew!

CHALLENGE:

Awards such as the one discussed above can have a positive impact on family, friends, etc. and provide a monetary piece that can be helpful to the recipient. Let me challenge you to consider a person(s) in your family that deserves such recognition. Then, give them that recognition!

21
Long Snap Demonstration

Adam had a very successful high school football career. We were so proud of him when he entered college. It took Adam five years and six summers to obtain his bachelor's degree in sociology. He did this despite documented learning disabilities, with dyslexia being the most noted challenge for him. For Adam to be eligible to play college division level II football, he had to obtain a minimum 2.0-grade point average after completing twelve college credits. This was required because he had a low score on his Scholastic Aptitude Test (SAT) exam. However, Adam was so driven to play college football that he worked very hard on the academic side of college. By the end of his first college semester, he obtained the required 2.0-grade point average. Thus he began playing college football in the fall of 1994.

One of the funniest academic experiences that Adam had was in a class called Fundamentals of Speech. Part of the requirement for the class was a three to five-minute demonstration speech to show how something worked. The student could pick the topic.

The day arrived for Adam to do his presentation speech. Off he went to class with his notes and a football in hand. The teacher invited Adam up to the front of the classroom. Adam proceeded to completely clean off the teacher's desk and then crawled up onto the desk. Standing up on the desk, he then turned his back toward the audience. He spread his feet far apart, bent over, and placed the football out in front of him while resting it on the desk. He was now in a position to deliver his speech back between his spread legs, i.e., "How to Long Snap a Football." The professor loved the speech, particularly the attention-getting aspect of it. He received an "A." As you can imagine, there was a tremendous amount of laughter.

GOD PROVIDED WISDOM

Hebrews 5:14 (TLB)**:** You will never be able to eat solid spiritual food and understand the deeper things of God's Word until you become better Christians and learn right from wrong by practicing doing right.

CHALLENGE:
Adam had football to motivate him to study and work hard in a learning environment. What motivates you to be motivated to study and learn God's Word?

22
Cal U—What a Game

Another vivid memory of Adam's college days involved a 1995 early season game against California University of Pennsylvania (Cal U). To set the stage, it was the Tuesday evening before the game at Cal U. I received a telephone call from Adam advising me that he was quitting the football team effective immediately. I realized this was not a conversation to have over the telephone. So, I told Adam I was leaving immediately for Bloomsburg, and we would go out for dinner.

When I first saw Adam, it was clear that he was emotionally upset. We went to a local Bloomsburg restaurant, and Adam began to dump everything on his mind. About fifteen minutes into the conversation, I realized the issue was an upperclassman beating down an underclassman.

The prior year as a freshman, Adam was on the taxi squad. As a taxi squad player, he was part of the team that ran the plays of the next week's opponent. Once these players became sophomores, they typically no longer had to fill that spot; new freshman players filled this role.

One of the seniors on the team began to ridicule Adam because he was still being used on the taxi squad. This upperclassman was saying things like: "You are still on the level of a JV player; you can't play with the big guys," etc. Adam was very competitive, and if he was going to ride the bench for another year, he was done with college football. I encouraged him not to make an immediate decision that he could regret. After further discussion, he decided to give his best at practice and in the game at Cal U that week and then make his decision.

All day Saturday, the day of the game, it rained and rained. And to top it off, Bloomsburg's offense stalled six times, requiring the ball be punted. Each snap was perfect. It was a very close game, and Bloomsburg came out on top.

After the game, as Pat and I were walking off the field, I was able to walk beside the senior player who was causing all the turmoil for Adam. I made sure he knew I was Adam's father, and he immediately started praising Adam for the perfect long snaps that he made in the game just completed.

Sunday evening, after the team viewed the Cal U game films, Adam called me. Man, was he ever excited. He was recognized as the outstanding special teams player for the Cal U game. This recognition and all the positive comments about his six perfect long snaps with a wet football had a very positive impact on Adam. I asked Adam if he still felt like quitting the team, to which he replied emphatically, "No way."

However, on the downside, Adam often experienced painful headaches following games. These headaches began almost immediately following a game and typically continued for several days. Following most home football games, we took Adam out for dinner. For the majority of the mealtime, Adam usually rested his elbow on the table and buried his head into his hand. When asked about this action, he would simply say, "I have a zinger; it is something I get after most every game."

GOD PROVIDED WISDOM

Today, traumatic brain injuries, chronic traumatic encephalopathy (CTE), as they are referred to, may be caused by injuries from many high-impact sports. The Mayo Clinic website indicates that CTE is the term used to describe brain degeneration likely caused by repeated head traumas. CTE is a diagnosis made only at autopsy by studying sections of the brain. CTE is a very rare disorder that is not yet well understood. CTE has a complicated relationship to head traumas such as post-concussion syndrome and second impact syndrome that occur earlier in life. Experts are still trying to understand how repeated head traumas—including how many head injuries and the severity of those injuries—and other factors might contribute to the changes in the brain that result in CTE.

Did Adam suffer from CTE? We will never know for sure. Due to the nature of his death causing injuries, an autopsy on his brain could not be performed.

CHALLENGE:
Review the entire Mayo Clinic website and learn more regarding CTE.

What impact/comments do the verses listed below have on your reaction to the knowledge we have on this subject?

Proverbs 3:7-8 (TLB): Don't be conceited, sure of your own wisdom. Instead, trust and reverence the Lord, and turn your back on evil; when you do that, then you will be given renewed health and vitality.

Proverbs 4:7 (TLB): Getting wisdom is the most important thing you can do! And with your wisdom, develop common sense and good judgment.

Proverbs 8:12 (TLB): Wisdom and good judgment live together, for wisdom knows where to discover knowledge and understanding.

Proverbs 28:26 (TLB): A man is a fool to trust himself! But those who use God's wisdom are safe.

Romans 11:33 (TLB): Oh, what a wonderful God we have! How great are his wisdom and knowledge and riches! How impossible it is for us to understand his decisions and his methods!

23
Mental Health (Schizophrenia)

Adam graduated from college in 1998. For several years, he worked as a probation and parole officer. It was while working in the Gettysburg correction system that he met Maura, and they were married in 2002. They seemed to be happily married for a little over a year when Adam began to say and do things that were not illegal but very unusual. This pattern of behavior began to snowball over a short period.

One Sunday afternoon in the fall of 2003, Adam was talking in a manner that did not make sense. His comments and actions were such that Maura became frightened. Maura encouraged Adam to call me, and he agreed. Later that afternoon, Adam and Maura called, and we discussed various topics, a number of them not following a logical path. In fact, if Maura had not been on the call, I would have wondered if he was under the influence of alcohol. He then stated that this was just one of the situations he was dealing with recently.

Although we were never able to medically confirm that Adam was Schizophrenic, characteristics and actions that he demonstrated from the summer of 2003 until his death in the fall of 2004 makes it extremely likely that he suffered from this debilitating disease.

The first time that I noticed "strange" actions on the part of Adam was in late 2003. Adam and I were discussing how things were going with his job. He did not hesitate to let me know that "everyone was out to get him." Initially, I thought that he was kidding. He very emphatically let me know that this was no laughing matter and should not be taken lightly.

See chapter 25, "Failed Petition 302," for further details.

GOD PROVIDED WISDOM

Through my research into these mental experiences involving Adam, I learned there are five primary mental illness diagnoses:

1. Major Depression

2. Schizophrenia

3. Bipolar Disorders

4. Alcohol Abuse

5. Obsessive-Compulsive Disorders

The Bible is an excellent resource when looking for ways to prevent mental illness. For example:

Positive Attitude: Philippians 4:8 (TLB): "And now, brothers, as I close this letter, let me say this one more thing: Fix your thoughts on what is true and good and right. Think about things that are pure and lovely, and dwell on the fine, good things in others. Think about all you can praise God for and be glad about."

Reining in feelings and emotions: Feelings and emotions come from God; see Genesis 1:27 (TLB): "So God made man like his Maker, like God, did God make man . . ." 1 John 4:8 (TLB) "But if a person isn't loving and kind, it shows that he doesn't know God—for God is love." Galatians 5:22-23 (TLB): "But when the Holy Spirit controls our lives He will produce this kind of fruit in us: love, joy, peace, patience, kindness, goodness, faithfulness, gentleness and self-control; and here there is no conflict with Jewish laws." Ephesians 5:18 (TLB): "Don't drink too much wine, for many evils lie along that path; be filled instead with the Holy Spirit and controlled by him."

Take Time Out: Watch the grass grow! Mark 6:31(TLB): "Then Jesus suggested, 'Let's get away from the crowds for a while and rest. For so many people were coming and going that they scarcely had time to eat.'" Exodus 20:10 (TLB): "But the seventh day is a day of Sabbath rest before the Lord your God . . ."

Too much change: need rest from this; Genesis 2:2 (TLB): "So on the seventh day, having finished his task, God ceased from this work he had been doing."

Confront fears: Proverbs 3:21-26 (TLB): "Have two goals: wisdom: that is, knowing and doing right; and common sense. Don't let them slip away, for they fill you with living energy, and are a feather in your cap. They keep you safe from defeat and disaster and from stumbling off the trail. With them on guard, you can sleep without fear; you need not be afraid of disaster or the plots of wicked men, for the Lord is with you; he protects you." 1 John 4:18 (TLB): "We need have no fear of someone who loves us perfectly; his perfect love for us eliminates all dread of what he might do to us. If we are afraid, it is for fear of what he might do to us and shows that we are not fully convinced that he really loves us."

Confront anxiety: our society is filled with anxiety - Psalm 4:4 (TLB): "Stand before the Lord in awe and do not sin against him. Lie quietly upon your bed in silent meditation."

Humor provides healing power: Proverbs 15:13 (TLB): "A happy face means a glad heart; a sad face means a breaking heart." Proverbs 17:22 (TLB): "Cheerful heart does well like medicine, but a broken spirit makes one sick."

Stay away from Dangerous Addictions: 1 Corinthians 6:12 (TLB): "I can do anything I want to if Christ has not said no, but some of these things aren't good for me. Even if I am allowed to do them, I'll refuse to if I think they might get such a grip on me that I can't easily stop when I want to."

Social Support System: Genesis 2:18 (TLB): "And the Lord God said, 'It isn't good for man to be alone; I will make a companion for him, a helper suited to his needs.'" Proverbs 27:17 (TLB): "A friendly discussion is as stimulating as the sparks that fly when iron strikes iron."

The resource used in locating verses was www.GotQuestions.org

Different Types of Schizophrenia and no one Common Characteristic Symptoms Include:

- Hallucinations-illusory perception
- Incoherence-lack of clarity or organization
- Delusions-mistaken or unfounded opinion or idea
- Catatonic Behavior-characterized by unresponsiveness or lack of movement
- Hyperactive Behavior-more engaged than abnormal.

App. for Involuntary Emergency Exam & Treatment (Mental Health Procedures Act of 1976 Section 302)

- Client can deny emergency help; petition designed to authorize the county to demand exam/admission
- County Mental Health Rep is looking for homicidal and/or suicidal tendencies.
- Petition allows for Involuntary Emergency Exam for person who has acted in a manner as to evidence inability to care for himself without supervision.

NOTE: protocols will vary from county to county.

CHALLENGE:

Which of the Bible passages listed above offer comfort to you?

24
Adam Travels to Oak Island, NC

In March 2004, for several days, I was trying to make telephone contact with Adam. I was leaving voicemail messages but received no response. Finally, on the morning of March 5th, I called Adam's employer. After a lengthy telephone discussion, Adam's supervisor told me that he had not seen Adam for several days and was also unaware of his current location.

I proceeded to make several calls and finally made contact with him. I began to ask Adam "20 questions" when he said, "Dad, they are out to get me. The people where I work are trying to set me up to fail." I was shocked at this comment and then asked what he meant. Adam attempted to explain it to me; however, I was not able to follow his logic. Our conversation was going in circles and getting nowhere fast. I asked him to meet me for lunch that same day so that we could continue our conversation. He agreed.

While we were together, Adam was very negative regarding his employment situation. He indicated that he was continually being put down and made to feel like a pile of crap. Everywhere he went, he felt like people were talking about him behind his back. Adam had gotten to the point where he was tired of being "crapped" upon and was going to move on and try a new avenue in life.—I'm sorry, but I must digress for a moment. This dialogue about being "crapped upon" reminds me of a recent experience that Jordan, Adam's cousin, had while deer hunting. Adam loved to deer hunt and would have enjoyed this story as told by Jordan:

I now live just over the line in Maryland and do some hunting around our house. In Maryland you are allowed to hunt on Sundays in some cases. Instead of setting the alarm for 7:30 and going to church with my wife and son like normal, I set it for 5:00 and was in my tree stand by 6. It was perfect. Cool. Calm, Easy to hear anything and everything that might be nearby. Just before daylight I heard something below me. As it got closer, I decided it sounded too small to be a deer and it was still too dark to see. Fox? Raccoon? Coyote? Bobcat? It got right under my tree stand and I could just barely make out jts shape. I think it is a raccoon and, in my head, hope he just keeps on moving along. The woods are full of trees, but I must have been in a special one. He walks right to the base and looks at it as if he might just want to climb it. At that point I decide to stand up. I stood up and he got scared. The problem was that his first instinct when startled was apparently to get to higher ground. He shot up my tree like a rocket. I yelled and jumped to the furthest point on my tree stand away from the tree that I could without falling. Now we are both stuck. He's stuck somewhere above me, and I'm stuck in my stand with what I'm convinced is a rabid beast about to pounce on me from above. Daylight came and I see it was a normal looking raccoon. I refuse to get down and risk screwing up the best time to see deer. I was constantly worried where he was and getting pelted with twigs as he scurried around above me. I conceded. I figured he wins. I got down, walked away 50 yards, and stood by a tree thinking to myself, "OK you won. Now get down and move along so we can both get on with our morning." It took five minutes, but he finally started down. I was satisfied until he got halfway down, picked a new limb and headed right back up. He finds a new crotch high in the tree and lays down . . . right above my tree stand. It was too nice a morning to quit so back up I climbed and decided he was comfy so I would just keep an eye on him. He would stay on his spot. I would stay at mine and we would co-exist for the morning. This worked for a while and truthfully would have continued to work if he wouldn't have been so noisy.

Every couple of minutes it seemed, I would hear noise above me and twigs and bark would fall on me. After about the third time, I looked up when I heard it. As I did, I was struck in the chin, shoulder, and thigh by the falling debris. The raccoon took a crap on me and apparently had been taking a crap on me for some time! Mad as I was, I almost had to laugh. He had won . . . game, set, match. I was done. I snapped a picture of him and packed up my things. It's his tree for the day. I should have gone to church!

Adam said he planned to start driving south on Route 95 and see where he ended up. Before Adam left the restaurant, we prayed together for his safety and guidance from the Holy Spirit.

Earlier that day, I purchased a telephone card that was activated with several hours of call time. I asked if he would please keep in touch with me. He said he would take the card but not make any promises to keep in touch.

Several weeks passed, and no one we knew heard a word from Adam. Finally, I received a call from Pat Cipala (Cindy's younger sister) indicating that she received a call from Adam. Adam was low on cash, and he recalled that he had a monetary gift coming from her for his birthday. Thus, Adam gave her his address, which was in Oak Island, North Carolina. Over the next few days, we learned the following:

- He quit his job as a probation officer;
- He is continuing with the divorce process involving Maura;
- He currently is living in North Carolina;
- He is working as a carpenter;
- Has cut ties with all family members.

As I thought about this information, the parable of the Prodigal Son took on a much more "real" meaning to me. Putting myself in the place of the father in this Biblical account caused me to realize the truths of love and forgiveness that Jesus was attempting to get across to His followers.

Things were again quiet for several weeks, with no communication involving Adam. Then, in June 2004, an Army recruiter called. This gentleman did his recruiting for the U. S. Army out of an office in Wilmington, North Carolina. Adam had been meeting with the recruiter and thus gave the recruiter permission to talk with me. The recruiter had one question: "Did Adam ever have a head injury when playing high school or college football?" "Yes," I said, "Adam had a concussion during his freshman year in high school." The only other information shared between the recruiter and me was that Adam applied for the position of Equipment Operator. Later in the application process, he was advised that he was unable to enlist in the U. S. Army because he failed the medical exam.

In late June 2004, Adam called with his voice filled with excitement! Adam told me that he was moving back to central Pennsylvania, and he asked if I would help him find a job. Adam also indicated that the Army enlistment idea fell through, and he needed to find a job in Pennsylvania. Adam then began to share some names of possible employers and asked if I would obtain application details. He further noted that he would be driving back home from North Carolina and expected to arrive home late in the week of July 15 to 19.

It was after midnight, on Saturday, July 10, 2004, when Pat and I settled down in bed for the night. Suddenly we heard the front door open and close. I looked over at Pat and said, "Did you lock the front door?"

Her response with a quiver in her voice was, "I think so!"

After a pause that seemed like hours, we heard footsteps from the stairway next to our bedroom. Then, our bedroom door swung open, and the silhouette of a very large man appeared in our doorway. I was about to try a loud shout scare tactic when the man said, "Hi dad, is it OK if I crash on your sofa for the night?"

After a long sigh of relief, I regained my composure and said, "Sure." I also said, "I thought that you were coming home at the end of next week?"

Adam said, "I was able to get an earlier start than originally thought." Adam then turned and went back downstairs.

I then turned to Pat and said, "Let's say a prayer of thanks to God for watching over Adam and keeping him safe." I then tried to sleep, but I knew it wasn't going to be possible. I told Pat I had to go down and talk with Adam—needless to say; I was wide awake! I wanted to ask him so many questions:

"Where have you been for the last several months?" I didn't give him a chance to answer, and I presented the next question, "Have you been working?" and the next question, "Why are you all of a sudden interested in getting a job?"

Then without hesitation, Adam said to me, "I have a son, and his name is Drew. He just turned 13, and I will meet him for the first time tomorrow."

I was overwhelmed in disbelief. I was shocked, confused, and angry. I never knew of my son Adam to lie to me directly. However, I was aware of the fact that there were times he did not tell me the whole story. Apparently, this was one of those stories where all the "pieces" had not been revealed. Adam said to me, "You remember Marion; well she is the mother of my child, Drew. I will be meeting Drew, now age thirteen, for the first time tomorrow."

Needless to say, I was quite concerned and emotional over this news. I had a grandson who was thirteen years old, and I never had an opportunity to participate in any of his first thirteen years of life. The concept of forgiveness became very real to me, not only toward my son, Adam, but also toward the child's mother, Marion. Adam and Marion kept me out of Drew's life. I was furious! Was this a story Adam made up? I decided that I would not say anything about this conversation to anyone until I had more facts. As it turned out, it was confirmed that Adam had a son, Drew. Drew lived in Selinsgrove with his mother and stepbrother.

GOD PROVIDED WISDOM

Read Luke 15:11-32 (TLB): The Parable of the Prodigal Son.

To further illustrate the point, he told them this story: "A man had two sons. When the younger son told his father, 'I want my share of your estate now, instead of waiting until you die,' his father agreed to divide his wealth between his sons.

A few days later, this younger son packed all his belongings and took a trip to a distant land, and there wasted all his money on parties and prostitutes. About the time his money was gone, a great famine swept over the land, and he began to starve. He persuaded a local farmer to hire him to feed his pigs. The boy became so hungry that even the pods he was feeding the swine looked good to him. And no one gave him anything.

When he finally came to his senses, he said to himself, "At home, even the hired men have food enough and to spare, and here I am, dying of hunger! I will go home to my father and say, 'Father, I have sinned against both heaven and you, and am no longer worthy of being called your son. Please take me on as a hired man.'"

So, he returned home to his father. And while he was still a long distance away, his father saw him coming, and was filled with loving pity and ran and embraced him and kissed him.

His son said to him, "Father, I have sinned against heaven and you, and am not worthy of being called your son"—But his father said to the slaves, "Quick! Bring the finest robe in the house and put it on him. And a jeweled ring for his finger, and shoes! And kill the calf we have in the fattening pen. We must celebrate with a feast, for this son of mine was dead and has returned to life. He was lost and is found." So, the party began.

Meanwhile, the older son was in the fields working; when he returned home, he heard dance music coming from the house, and he asked one of the servants what was going on. "Your brother is back," he was told, "and your father has killed the calf we were fattening and has prepared a great feast to celebrate his coming home again, unharmed."

The older brother was angry and wouldn't go in. His father came out and begged him, but he replied, "All these years I've worked hard for you and never once refused to do a single thing you told me to, and in all that time you never gave me even one young goat for a feast with my friends. Yet when this son of yours comes back after spending your money on prostitutes, you celebrate by killing the finest calf we have on the place."

"Look, dear son," his father said to him, "you and I are very close, and everything I have is yours. But it is right to celebrate. For he is your brother, and he was dead and has come back to life! He was lost and is found!"

CHALLENGE:

Did you have a time in your life where you ran away? If so, what age where you? Where did you go? How long did you stay? What did you learn? In the passage from Luke 15:11-32 (TLB), did you agree with the older son? (why or why not?)

25
Filed Petition 302

On September 4, 2004, Justin and I were at Mount St. Mary's College in Maryland at a Mid Penn ACES baseball tournament. My wife, Pat, stayed at home with Adam and our three younger sons, Landon, 15; Kaleb, 10; and Marcus, 1. Late that afternoon, Pat contacted the Dauphin County Crisis Intervention office due to Adam's "scary" interaction with them. She spoke to Miss Amanda from the Dauphin County Crisis Intervention office. Pat summarized Adam's actions: For most of the day, Adam sat outside in a lawn chair staring over the backyard, and at one point, he told Kaleb to ask his friends to stop talking about him. Adam also told Landon to tell Justin, 17, to tell his friends not to come to our house playing loud music on their car radio. Adam made numerous other such unusual comments. Kaleb began to cry; Landon began to get tears in his eyes; Kaleb said, "I just want the old Adam back!"

Because of Adam's unusual behavior, Pat decided that they needed to leave our home while waiting for Justin and me to return from the baseball tournament. Pat was concerned Adam may be at the point where he would harm someone. Pat, Marcus, Kaleb, and Landon left our home at about 6:30 P.M. Pat asked Miss Amanda if Crisis Intervention of Dauphin County could help? Amanda said they could come to our house if we wanted them to. Pat said she needed to discuss this with me. Miss Amanda said she would call back later.

At about 8:00 P.M., Miss Amanda called to gather more information. Pat gave her Adam's name, age, address, phone number, and the fact that

Adam was 6'5" and 240 lbs. Pat indicated that Adam said earlier that day that he wasn't currently suicidal or homicidal but had thoughts of suicide in the last week. Pat noted to Miss Amanda that Adam said the newscasters on TV were making fun of him, and the radio announcers could tell how he responded to the music they played; therefore, he would no longer listen to the radio. Miss Amanda ended the conversation noting if we wanted Crisis Intervention to come out and evaluate Adam, that we should call them.

Justin and I were driving home from the tournament when Pat called and said that she left the house with the boys because she was uncomfortable. He did not threaten them, but his comments and actions were affecting the boys, and she decided to leave; she had concern for their safety. At the time of this call, they were at the home of friends, and she was attempting to contact a Pennsylvania state trooper friend of ours who was aware of the challenges we were experiencing with Adam.

I advised Pat to stay at our friend's home until Justin and I arrived. In the meantime, I called Adam's college football coach to obtain the telephone number of Adam's line coach. In the discussions that followed, we felt that Coach Brian would be the best person to try to talk to Adam regarding the need for medical intervention in his situation.

At this time, Justin and I arrived at the home where Pat and our other sons were staying. We decided that Justin and I would go to our home and act as if we were just getting home from Maryland, interact with Adam, and consider calling Coach Brian. Pat made me aware of her conversations with Dauphin County Crisis Intervention and the information they provided to her. I said that I might contact them if needed once I interacted with Adam.

Justin and I went to our home around 9:00 P.M. Adam was sitting in a lawn chair at the west edge of our property, looking up into the sky. I asked Adam about Pat and the boys. He said he didn't know where they went. I talked with Adam about our day of baseball and was sorry he decided not to go with us. I told Adam that if he would have gone to Maryland with Justin and me that day, I was going to discuss with him the idea of getting in touch with Coach Brian to discuss the concerns he had been expressing (i.e., people blinking at him, people mocking him, people following him, etc.).

Adam always had high regard for Coach Brian, and I thought a conversation with him would be helpful. I further expressed to Adam that since he didn't go with us to Maryland, I called Coach Brian anyway and discussed his willingness to speak to Adam. Coach Brian agreed and, in fact, is at home right now and would love to talk to him. So, I asked Adam if it was OK for me to call Coach Brian and let him talk to him. Adam indicated that he was fine and that he didn't want to talk to Coach Brian.

I called Coach Brian and updated him on the situation. Coach Brian asked me to let him know if Adam changed his mind. I went back outside and engaged in further conversation with Adam. I indicated that, as he knew, we had been discussing for a week now the importance of obtaining medical intervention. I reminded him that he didn't like the feelings he was having (in his words), and I reminded him of the information I obtained from the medical personnel about going to the Hershey Medical Center. I asked Adam again if he would go with Justin and me to the Hershey Medical Center. He indicated, "Dad, I am fine!"

"Adam," I said, "If you are not willing to go talk with medical personnel, then I will need to call and have medical personnel come to our home."

Adam's comment was, "Dad, this conversation is over!"

I called Dauphin County Crisis Intervention and left a message for a return call. I was advised that the persons on duty were currently working on a case in another part of Dauphin County. Miss Amanda returned my call and confirmed that she was aware of the call my wife made earlier in the day. I updated Miss Amanda on what was taking place, i.e., unusual behavior patterns of that day and evening, the fact that my wife and sons were not comfortable to be in Adam's presence, the fact that Pat and our sons were at a friend's home now, etc. Miss Amanda indicated that they were tied up with another case right now and weren't sure how long it would take. She asked if the situation could wait until the next day (Sunday morning). I indicated that I was not comfortable waiting that long. Amanda indicated that she would see how things went with the case they were currently on and call me back. I called my Pennsylvania State Police friend and advised him of the latest developments. He said that he would alert the Lykens barracks of the State Police with appropriate information in case their intervention was needed.

A short while later, Miss Amanda called back and said they could come. She discussed the procedure they would follow (State Police would accompany her, and she would interact with Adam to assess if an intervention was appropriate). She also explained that there is a process involving a petition 302, where an immediate family member can complete documentation regarding unusual behavior and actions and have the person involuntarily committed for medical evaluation. Their estimated ETA was sometime after 10:00 P.M.

I called and updated my Pennsylvania state trooper friend. He said that he would follow-up with the Lykens barracks of the State Police regarding details on Adam's vehicle description, license number, etc., in case he tries to run when the Crisis Intervention people arrive. He also advised me that if I had access to Adam's vehicle keys, I should hide them.

Miss Amanda and Miss Amy from the Dauphin County Crisis unit arrived at our home at 10:15 P.M. With them were two uniformed Pennsylvania State Police troopers. When they arrived, Adam was on the sofa in the family room, and Justin was upstairs.

Upon arriving, Miss Amanda asked where Adam was, and I indicated he was on the sofa in the family room. Miss Amanda, Miss Amy, and one of the troopers went in to talk with Adam; the other trooper stayed with me in the hall, and Justin remained upstairs. I could hear the conversation in the family room.

Miss Amanda asked Adam how he was feeling. Adam said, "I am sorry that you had to come out this evening, but I am not going to be able to talk with you. However, I want to tell you one thing. I am not homicidal, and I am not suicidal."

Adam went to get up, and I heard the trooper say, "Please sit down!"

Adam responded by saying, "Yes, sir, I will do whatever you say, I don't want any problems."

Miss Amanda came out to tell us that basically, Adam won't talk with her, so she is therefore unable to assess him for the need for intervention. I asked Amanda if it was OK for me to enter into a conversation with Adam; Miss Amanda indicated that would be fine.

At this point, all of us, except Justin, were in the family room. The conversation went as follows: I reminded Adam of our many discussions during the past week and how he was upset with people on television, mocking him, people blinking at him, people following him, etc., and noted that we discussed advice from other medical professionals. I noted our efforts to take him to the Hershey Medical Center.

Adam's response was, "Dad, I'm fine, and you shouldn't have bothered these fine people to come out here tonight."

I again reminded Adam of his earlier comments about not feeling well and that he even mentioned approximately a week ago that he may have to harm himself—his general response again was, "Dad, I'm fine."

I then told Adam that I understood there is a process called a petition 302 where I can complete it and have him involuntarily admitted for evaluation. I looked at Miss Amanda and Miss Amy, and they acknowledged that I was correct. I turned to Adam and said, "Adam, I am going to ask you one more time to go with Justin and me to Hershey Medical Center. However, if you refuse again, I am going to complete the paperwork involved in the petition 302 process and have you involuntarily admitted for evaluation. This is a thing called 'tough love,' and I need to do it because I love you."

Adam responded to me by saying, "Dad, you need to do what you need to do."

I asked Adam one more time if he would go with Justin and me to Hershey Medical Center, and he said, "Dad, I am fine." Adam listened while I told him I had no other choice but to complete the petition 302 paperwork and have him involuntarily admitted for evaluation. I was then given the paperwork and guided through the completion process—this took about 20 minutes. When completed, Miss Amy asked if she could use our phone to call a county official. I responded with yes.

One of the State Police troopers than advised me that I might want to put some personal belongings of Adam's in a case to take along to the hospital. The trooper explained that an ambulance would be called and it would be good for us to follow them to the Hershey Medical Center because the medical personnel will want to speak to us.

I went upstairs and began to get Adam's items collected and placed in a gym bag. While still upstairs, one of the troopers called and said, "Mr. Reitz, would you please come downstairs." I came down, and Miss Amy advised me that the "request has been denied."

"Excuse me," I emphatically stated.

Miss Amy said, "I called a county official, and the request for involuntary admission has been denied."

I said, "I previously understood you to say that if I completed the petition 302, Adam would be taken involuntarily for evaluation."

All Miss Amy said was, "I'm sorry the request has been denied, and there is nothing more for us to do but leave."

"I have a very deep appreciation for the difficulty of your job," I said," "However," I continued, "What do I do now?" All four began to walk outside to leave. I followed them. Once outside, I asked, "What am I suppose to do now? I have a son inside who needs medical intervention. I have a son upstairs, who is confused and concerned. I don't know how Adam is going to react to this past discussion with you. I have a wife and two sons who are confused, in tears, because of some of Adam's comments."

Miss Amy said, "You can consider filing a court order on Tuesday (the day after the Labor Day holiday)."

I asked, "In other words, this is a document where a judge would decide on whether the medical intervention was needed?"

She responded, "Yes."

Then I asked, "What do I do in the meantime?" No further advice was provided, and they got in their vehicles and headed down our driveway!

GOD PROVIDED WISDOM

We also learned through this process of involving the County Mental Health Agency that one may have to deal with multiple County Mental Health Agencies. The determining jurisdiction factor, at any point in time, is the County of residence.

Adam was residing in three different counties during the summer of 2004. Some of the time, he was in Dauphin County (our home); some of the time, he was in Northumberland County (staying with a close friend from high school); some of the time, he was in Cumberland County (where his wife Maura resided). Although it was good to have an agency in the geographic area involved when issues arose, we found out the agencies did not have a standard protocol for handling the 302 petition.

After Adam's death, I had conversations with all three county agencies. I was told by Northumberland County that had the scenario I shared with them taken place in Northumberland County, the completed 302 petition would have been accepted and put into action; i.e., Adam would have been committed to a medical facility for evaluation.

CHALLENGE:

Research the mental health facilities in your geographic area. Learn what their emphasis for treatment is: children, adults, men, women, etc. Through discussion and prayer, find ways that you can support their work if it so warrants. As you conduct this research, remember, Job 28:17 (TLB), "Wisdom is far more valuable than gold and glass. It cannot be bought for jewels mounted in fine gold." Also, keep in mind, Psalm 16:7 (TLB) "I will bless the Lord who counsels me; he gives me wisdom in the night. He tells me what to do."

26
God is Faithful

"God is Faithful." Let me share a personal struggle when I questioned God's faithfulness.

On the Thursday before Adam's death, I spent three and one-half hours on the telephone with numerous professional persons trying to obtain the needed medical intervention for Adam. By noon I was frustrated, upset, and confused. I went to God in prayer and said: "I turn it over to you, God; I have exhausted every avenue I can imagine; please watch over Adam and get him the medical intervention he needs!"

The next day, Friday, I spent the day in fasting and prayer, repeating the request, through prayer, that I made the day before. The next day, Saturday, I received a telephone call telling me that my son Adam was dead. My initial reaction was, "God, you failed me; God, you were not faithful to your word and teachings."

I am sure every person reading this account can relate to an event or series of events, where you fervently prayed to God for His intervention, and the outcome of the event(s) were not as you requested. Your reaction was, "God, you failed me; God, you were not faithful to your word and teachings; God, if you are a God of love, how could you let this happen.

God never calls us to do anything without faithfully keeping His word and enabling us to do it. We are not always faithful to God, but He remains faithful to us.

Consider the Old Testament account of when the children of Israel were led out of Egypt only to be stopped by the Red Sea. It seemed that

God had abandoned His promise to them. The sea was barring their advance, and the murderous Egyptian army was racing to overtake them! Yet God proved then, as he always has, that He is absolutely faithful to every word He speaks to His children. Listen closely to Moses' summary of what God does for us when He is leading us into the unknown. "Don't be afraid! The Lord God is your leader, and He will fight for you with His mighty miracles, just as you saw Him do in Egypt. And you know how He has cared for you again and again here in the wilderness, just as a father cares for his child!" (Deuteronomy 1: 29b-32a).

We need to remember that God may have spoken to us through His Word about something in particular, such as joining a ministry in our church, leading a small group Bible study, finding a new job, or perhaps ending a personal relationship that went bad. We have obeyed Him, but now we face a vast untransferable sea. It seems that God will not do what we thought He would.

God is faithful, and that's our guarantee. We can keep walking confidently into the unknown because our Father is committed to direct us as to where to step next, to carry us when we can't go any farther, to provide us with protection from harm and to care for us, providing for every need. He has called us. He'll do it! So no matter how dark the path ahead looks, no matter how scared we feel, we just need to grab ahold of our Father's hand and just keep walking in the direction that He's leading, even if we don't understand everything that is going on! Regardless of how bleak our present circumstances are or how uncertain our future seems, we cannot lose hope. No one has ever experienced unfaithfulness on God's part! We need to allow time for God to reveal His faithfulness to us.

I came across an article that provides a vivid example of what we have been discussing. The article quotes a London newspaper: "Men wanted for hazardous journey. Small wages, bitter cold, long months of complete darkness, constant danger, and safe return doubtful." The advertisement was written by Sir Ernest Shackleton, the famous South Pole explorer.

Now, returning to my comments made earlier about God "not being faithful" in answering my prayers of deliverance for Adam, I am reminded today that God did not even spare His own Son on that first Good Friday of long ago. So, why should I be surprised that God did not spare my son on that Friday in September 2004?

The thing that we need to focus upon when dealing with the "trials of life" is "how does God want to demonstrate His faithfulness through us? How does he want us to carry His cross." Not focusing on the things that we don't understand, for example, my son Adam's untimely death, but rather allowing God to work through our circumstances of life in a way that demonstrates our faithfulness to carry His cross and allow Him to work in His mysterious ways through our committed lives so that His will be done!

God is faithful, even though we don't understand many events. Our response to God needs to be "Thy will be done," even in those events of life that we don't understand. The ultimate result will then demonstrate the fact that "God is Faithful!" The key point is that we have got to get off "whys" that impede us and get onto the "whats" that empower us!

GOD PROVIDED WISDOM

I am reminded of Jesus' words in Matthew 16:24 (TLB): "Then Jesus said to the disciples, "If anyone wants to be a follower of mine, let him deny himself and take up his cross and follow me." The Lord was calling people to go with Him on a hazardous journey, i.e., the way of the cross. He issued that call after telling His disciples that He was going to Jerusalem to suffer and be killed.

CHALLENGE:
Read and pray over the verses below from John 17 (TLB). Truly God is Faithful, and so is Jesus. May we remain faithful to them; this is our challenge!

John 17:1-5 (TLB) **(Jesus prays for Himself):** "When Jesus had finished saying all these things, he looked up to heaven and said, 'Father, the time has come. Reveal the glory of your Son so that he can give the glory back to you. For you have given authority over every man and woman in all the earth. He gives eternal life to each one you have given Him. And this is the way to have eternal life—by knowing you, the only true God, and Jesus

Christ, the one you sent to earth! I brought glory to you here on earth by doing everything you told me to. And now, Father, reveal my glory as I stand in your presence, the glory we shared before the world began.'"

John 17:6-19 (TLB) (Jesus prays for His disciples): "I have told these men all about you. They were in the world, but then you gave them to me. Actually, they were always yours, and you gave them to me; and they have obeyed you. Now they know that everything I have is a gift from you, for I have passed on to them the commands you gave me; and they accepted them and know of a certainty that I came down to earth from you, and they believe you sent me.

"My plea is not for the world but for those you have given me because they belong to you. And all of them, since they are mine, belong to you; and you have given them back to me with everything else of yours, and so *they are my glory.* Now I am leaving the world, and leaving them behind, and coming to you. Holy Father, keep them in your own care—all those you have given me—so that they will be united just as we are, with none missing. During my time here, I have kept safe within your family all of these you gave me. I guarded them so that not one perished, except the son of hell, as the Scriptures foretold.

"And now I am coming to you. I have told them many things while I was with them so that they would be filled with my joy. I have given them your commands. And the world hates them because they don't fit in with it, just as I don't. I'm not asking you to take them out of the world, but to keep them safe from Satan's power. They are not part of this world any more than I am. Make them pure and holy through teaching them your words of truth. As you sent me into the world, I am sending them into the world, and I consecrate myself to meet their need for growth in truth and holiness.

John 17:20-26 (TLB) (Jesus prays for all future believers): "I am not praying for these alone but also for the future believers who will come to me because of the testimony of these. My prayer for all of them is that they will be of one heart and mind, just as you and I are, Father—that just as you are in me and I am in you, so they will be in us, and the world will believe you sent me. "I have given them the glory you gave me—the glorious unity of being one, as we are—I in them and you in me, all being perfected into one—so that the world will know you sent me and will understand that you love them as much as you love me. Father, I want them with me—these you've given me—so that they can see my glory. You gave me the glory because you loved me before the world began!"

"O, righteous Father, the world doesn't know you, but I do, and these disciples know you sent me. And I have revealed you to them and will keep on revealing you so that the mighty love you have for me may be in them, and I in them."

Bottom line: God loves us as much as He loves His own Son, Jesus!

27
Promoted to Heaven

Psalm 33:14 notes that from His dwelling place God watches all who are on earth. I believe God was very much aware of Adam and his challenges and needs.

As our children grew, my wife and I talked about what it meant to have your sins forgiven. We introduced them to John 3:16 (KJV), "For God so loved the world that He gave His only begotten Son that who so ever believes in Him shall not perish but have everlasting life." When Adam was a pre-teen, I had discussions with him regarding this topic. I am comfortable that he accepted Jesus as his Lord and Savior at that time.

The drawing to the right is how I picture Adam as he left earth with its sadness, anger, illness, frustration, confusion, etc. and into the accepting, caring, loving arms of God.

It was on September 11, 2004, that Adam made this trip to meet God. The news came to me late in the evening by telephone. I was devastated. I was lost for words, and I told my family that I needed to leave and would be back shortly. This was a big mistake because I left my family uninformed and confused for a while.

All I could do was think of talking with my pastor, Reverend George Barto. I was able to drive to his home in ten minutes. Upon arriving, I shared what I knew, and we had a prayer. Reverend Barto asked about Pat and the children. When I told him what I did, he said that we needed to go back and be with them. So, Reverend Barto and his wife Suella drove to our home. Upon arrival, I apologized to my family for leaving abruptly without telling them about Adam's death.

Reverend and Suella Barto provided reassuring words in a manner in which only they could do. After a time of prayer, the Bartos returned home, and Pat and I held our children, trying to comfort them. Even though I was comfortable with Adam's eternal status, the human element of Adam no longer alive and physically with us was devastating!

As you can imagine, there was virtually no sleeping that night for Pat and me. We still had not met our grandson, Drew. From July 11, 2004 (the date Adam returned from North Carolina), until September 11, 2004 (Adam's date of death), every time we asked Adam, "When do we get to meet Drew?" He said, "The timing is not right yet."

All we knew was Drew and his mother lived somewhere in the Selinsgrove, Pennsylvania, area. After making a few early morning telephone calls, we were able to obtain a telephone number for Marion. I called and asked her to stay home because Pat and I would be there in about two hours. Not wanting to drive following a sleepless night, I contacted a close friend, Dave Mongold, to drive us to Selinsgrove. Dave was immediately ready, with no questions asked. Within an hour, we were at the street address in Selinsgrove that Marion provided.

During the ride to Selinsgrove, Pat and I sat in the back seat of the car and cried, hugged, prayed, slept, and discussed how to handle our first encounter with the teenager who we believed was our grandson. We decided that after greeting and hugging Drew and Marion, Pat would stay at the apartment with Drew while Marion and I walked around town, enabling her to talk freely.

As we pulled into the apartment complex, Marion and Drew came out and stood on the porch. One glimpse of Drew left virtually no doubt in our minds that this thirteen-year-old young man was Adam's son, our grandson. As Pat and I gathered our emotions, I said to Pat and Dave that this young man was the "spitting" image of Adam when Adam was thirteen years old. Once we got out of the car, Pat and I walked to Drew, and he greeted us in a very polite and engaging manner. We spoke briefly, and then I asked Drew if he would be willing to stay at the apartment with Pat while his mother and I went for a walk. Drew said that would be OK.

Marion and I walked around the streets of Selinsgrove for about two hours. I presented many questions to her, and she talked very freely and openly. Marion expressed thoughts about raising a second child and why she would prefer to raise the child herself. Everything that Marion said was consistent with what limited knowledge I had. There was no reason to believe she was anything but honest and forthcoming. After months of dealing with half-truths, lies, and deception, I was grateful to Marion for her honesty.

I told Marion of Adam's death. From her shocked and emotional reaction, I was sure that she was not aware of it. As expected, she had many "why" questions. She expressed disbelief and talked about many interactions that Adam and Drew recently experienced. She noted that Adam bought Drew his football shoes needed for the upcoming football season. Adam talked extensively about being the dad in the future that he should have been in the past. All of this information made me realize how difficult it was going to be to tell Drew about his father's death.

After sharing the facts of Adam's death with Drew, he, too, did not believe what he was being told. Drew told us that Adam told him of people who were out to get him. Therefore, Drew concluded that these people must have killed his dad. Throughout the discussion, there was much emotion. However, again as experienced with Marion, there were many "why" questions. After a considerable amount of time attempting to convey partial answers to Drew, we prayed seeking God's wisdom and direction as we moved forward with our lives.

As expected, Pat and I would have to face what would seem like an endless ride back to Halifax. Dave's help driving and emotional support on this challenging day were fantastic! An even longer road ahead of us was the needed "healing process" that would require much in the way of forgiveness. Forgiveness, we, as a new family unit, would need to experience. Very clearly, we would need God's guidance as we worked our way beyond this tragedy!

GOD PROVIDED WISDOM

Following are verses related to the topic of being promoted to heaven:

- **John 3:16-17 (TLB):** "For God loved the world so much that he gave his only Son so that anyone who believes in him shall not perish but have eternal life. God did not send his Son into the world to condemn it, but to save it."

- **Romans 3:23 (TLB):** "Yes, all have sinned; all fall short of God's glorious ideal . . ."

- **Romans 6:23 (TLB):** "For the wages of sin is death, but the gift of God is eternal life through Jesus Christ our Lord."

- **1 Corinthians 15:1-4 (TLB):** "Now let me remind you, brothers, of what the Gospel really is, for it has not changed—it is the same Good News I preached to you before. You welcomed it then and still do now, for your faith is squarely built upon this wonderful message, and it is this Good News that saves you if you still firmly believe it, unless, of course, you never really believed it in the first place. I passed on to you right from the first what had been told to me, that Christ died for our sins just as the Scriptures said he would, and that he was buried, and that three days afterward, he arose from the grave just as the prophets foretold."

CHALLENGE:

Virtually everyone in our world today indicates we must earn everything we receive. The above verses are sending the exact opposite message, i.e., being promoted to heaven cannot be earned. It is a gift from God. By His grace, we are set FREE! May you be vigilant in understanding and appreciating this gift provided through the death and resurrection of God's Son,

Jesus! Once you accept Jesus as your Savior, you are further challenged to read and study the Bible to see how you can follow God's teachings and share these teachings with others.

Now, if you have committed your life to God and accepted Jesus as your Savior, write a list of several of the teachings in the Bible on which you are currently focused. Also, list how you are attempting to share these teachings with others.

28
The Tattoo Provides Closure

Back during his college days, Adam obtained a large tattoo on his right lower leg. When he came home the weekend following obtaining the tattoo, he was sure to wear shorts so all the world could see. Adam knew that I was not a fan of tattoos, so he was anxious to see how I would respond.

It wasn't long until one of his younger brothers noticed the tattoo. Immediately Adam said, "Dad, I know you don't approve of tattoos, but this design is very special to me. What makes it so special to me is that mom and I are the only persons who know what the design means."

I responded, "Then it certainly is special." As it turned out, this tattoo had further special significance in the future that no one anticipated. Let me explain. Following the completion of Adam's mother's autopsy report, we learned that all major bones in Cindy's body were broken as a result of the accident. In addition, her injuries were so severe in other ways that it was recommended her body not be viewed by the public. Our children, being very young, had little they could do but accept the fact that their mother was in the casket. Even though they wanted to believe us, human nature is such that they wanted to have visual closure that their mother's body was in the casket. Since closure was not obtained, in the future, the kids would question (hope) that mom was somehow still alive. For example, on occasions, our one child would rush to open the door when the doorbell rang because they were hoping that mom would be there.

Following Adam's death, we had a similar situation because of the nature of his injuries; he could not be viewed. We focused on the closure issues experienced in Cindy's death and came up with a way to complete the closure issues for Adam's case.

Below is a picture of the tattoo that Adam had placed on his right calf. It was clear to me that anybody who knew Adam would have at some point in time seen the tattoo. Therefore, the funeral director covered Adam's body from the waist and up, thus enabling the tattoo to be visible and viewed. As a result, there were no closure issues.

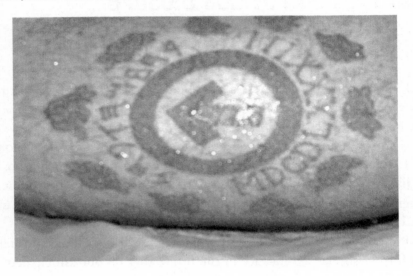

GOD PROVIDED WISDOM

Drew was raised in a non-traditional fashion. However, his mother was dedicated to her role as a caring mother, seeking God's wisdom. Drew had a positive school experience in both middle school and high school. He participated in extracurricular programs and excelled, especially in football. Upon graduation from high school, he experienced one year of college and several different employment experiences in the world of employee safety.

CHALLENGE:
When you were raised, who made up your family? Make a list of the relationships and the lack of relationships that you dealt with. Did you have

special relationships with people outside your immediate family that were important to you? Were there Bible verses that helped you deal with the emotions involved? Did you have any persons whom you could discuss such issues?

29
Remembrance

At the time of the death of a loved one, it is essential to allow people to express their feelings. In our case, we made this opportunity available to guests attending the Celebration of Life service for our 29-year old son. As people entered the church for the viewing or service, a sheet of paper and pen were provided with the following instruction:

PRECIOUS MEMORIES: the family of Adam Reitz wants to put together a memory book. They ask you to share a memory you have of him. Adam's life/ memories may stimulate others to become disciples for Jesus Christ.

Please write and sign the remembrance in the space below. Place the completed sheet of paper in the basket provided or leave it in the pew following the service. Thank you for sharing.

This exercise successfully provided guests with a way to gather together some of their thoughts and emotions. They quietly began to giggle among themselves as they shared memories and spent quality time writing them down.

See Appendix A for several examples of the 65 papers that were turned in at the end of the Celebration of Life Service.

The Singing Benediction

Another idea to use when conducting a Celebration of Life service is to re-write the words to the well-known Sunday school song "I've Got a Home in Glory Land." Use this re-written song as the benediction (Yes, I sing solo). My instructions presented to the congregation are: "Please close your eyes and envision your loved one standing in the clouds. Your loved one has a message for you, and they are going to convey the message through the song."

Using this song puts a very positive focus on the end of the service. Also, give a typed copy of the words to the family; it is a great conversation piece for use when a person is not sure what to say.

See Appendix B for an example of a singing benediction written for use at my Celebration of Life Service.

95 Facts

One more idea for "Remembering Your Loved One." My father lived to the age of ninety-five. Thus we had a project for many members of our family, gathering the facts and putting together the booklet. We then distributed the booklet upon entry to the church. It gave people something to read while standing in that long line. Also, it provided guests additional information to discuss with the family of the deceased.

See Appendix C for the example used in my father's service.

CHALLENGE:
The next Celebration of Life service you attend, offer to do the following:

Write a Benediction to the tune of "I've Got a Home in Glory Land;" present the idea to the pastor and family of the deceased; offer to sing the Benediction.

30
Forgiveness is a MUST

There are a number of examples of forgiveness that are recorded in the Bible. For example, the first human beings, Adam and Eve, were also the first humans to sin. They were also the first to experience God's forgiveness. Given the freedom to choose to obey God, Adam and Eve opted for rebellion. Yet God pursued them and made a way for the human race to experience forgiveness.

Another example is when an angry Moses murdered an Egyptian slave master. Despite this horrible sin, God used Moses to rescue His enslaved people. A convicted criminal who was crucified with Jesus on the cross cried out to Jesus and was welcomed into Paradise by Jesus because of his sincere request to be forgiven.

These examples of forgiveness remind me of my struggles involving this subject as it relates to forgiving Adam and Marion. Their desire to have it their way resulted in me having no part in the first 13 years of Drew's life.

Then, because of Drew's interest in meeting his biological father, Marion put forth efforts to locate Adam, which resulted in her locating Adam in Oak Island, North Carolina. It wasn't long after these events that Adam decided to return to Pennsylvania, doing so in mid-July 2004. And as you read earlier, two months later, on September 16, 2004, we were conducting his Celebration of Life service.

September 16th was a long day, and everyone involved in the service did a wonderful job of bringing honor and glory to our Lord and Savior

Jesus Christ. Also, the many remembrances of Adam's life helped work through the grieving process.

About 10:00 P.M. that same evening, I received a telephone call from Marion. When I answered the phone, I could tell that she was crying heavily. It was evident from her comments that some of her past actions were weighing heavily upon her heart. One person who she indicated was really weighing heavy upon her heart was me. Marion expressed how upset she was with herself regarding decisions she made that eventually were detrimental to Adam. Marion said, "Will you forgive me? I am sorry. Please forgive me!"

Although I was quite upset with Marion and had been for some time now, I also was a Christian. I knew if I didn't forgive Marion, the Lord God Almighty would not forgive me for my past, present, and future sins.

The result is that I forgave Marion, and I realized that the only way I was able to do so was because of my knowledge of the power of the Holy Spirit within me.

GOD PROVIDED WISDOM

God's teachings are clear:

- We all need a Savior to forgive us;

- We need to be ready to forgive others;

- There is no limit on the number of times we should be ready to forgive;

- We must be prepared to seek forgiveness daily;

- I praise God that He gave me the ability to forgive Marion at this challenging crossroads in her life.

At this time, another Biblical story comes to mind. King David saw a woman bathing, and he immediately wanted her. Even though the woman, Bathsheba, was the wife of one of David's soldiers, Uriah, David took her away. When David learned that she was pregnant, he panicked and arranged for Uriah to be moved to the front lines, where his likelihood of death was more probable. Soon after this move, Uriah was killed in battle.

Jesus conquered the grave.

By God's grace, David was forgiven when he sincerely sought God's redemption (forgiveness). Yes, David was forgiven and moved on to be a key person in God's plan of salvation for all people. However, as is always the case, there were severe consequences for David because of his sin.

The death and resurrection of Jesus proved that the grave has been conquered.

- All have sinned;

- Christ died for all who seek and accept Him;

- All can be saved who believe in Jesus and ask for His forgiveness;

- All who have been forgiven are expected to forgive others.

CHALLENGE:

Through prayer this coming week, identify one person who you need to forgive. Then call them up and express your desire to forgive them. When completed with this task, you will feel SUPER!

31
DNA Fiasco

For nine months following Adam's death, many unanswered questions remained. Many of these questions dealt with the subject of DNA testing. DNA stands for deoxyribonucleic acid. It's the genetic code that determines all the characteristics of a living thing. Your DNA is what makes you, you! Nobody else in the world will have DNA the same as you unless you have an identical twin. Deoxyribonucleic acid is a large molecule in the shape of a double helix. That's somewhat like a ladder that's been twisted many times.

DNA testing results were of great interest to me because it was recognized as the sure way to determine who the surviving parents of a person are. We were looking for this assurance in two areas, (1) if Drew was Adam's son and (2) if Marion was Drew's mother. If this were true, then Marion would be eligible for survivor benefits from Social Security to assist her in raising Drew until he obtained the age of eighteen. Secondly, if Adam had Schizophrenia, confirmation would be beneficial for future members of the family lineage.

The initial tests found no DNA. One of the critical issues surrounding the DNA questions dealt with whether the blood samples extracted from Adam's body were appropriately transported. This seemed to be the critical issue because the reputable laboratory that we selected to perform needed lab analysis determined that the initial blood samples sent to them were not viable (i.e., no DNA was found). Since this was considered a very unusual outcome in DNA testing, additional experts were brought into the case.

Remaining blood samples from gray top tubes were available at a lab in Willow Grove, Pennsylvania. These samples were remaining from tests done at the Willow Grove lab (i.e., a standard legal procedure in cases such as Adam's), checking to see if the presence of drugs or alcohol were in the body of the deceased. Fortunately, these blood samples were useable, and our parenting questions were answered.

GOD PROVIDED WISDOM

Matthew 26:27–29 (TLB): "And he took a cup of wine and gave thanks for it and gave it to them and said, 'Each one drink from it, for this is my blood, sealing the new covenant. It is poured out to forgive the sins of multitudes. Mark my words—I will not drink this wine again until the day I drink it new with you in my Father's Kingdom.'"

John 6:53 (TLB): "So Jesus said it again, 'With all the earnestness I possess I tell you this: Unless you eat the flesh of the Messiah and drink his blood, you cannot have eternal life within you.'"

John 6:54 (TLB): "But anyone who does eat my flesh and drink my blood has eternal life, and I will raise him at the Last Day."

Challenge:

Per the use of wine to represent the shed blood of Jesus Christ, the plan of salvation is made available to all man-kind (see verses listed above). Read these verses to learn more about the saving power through the shed blood of Jesus.

As it relates to our physical world today, read an article from a well-known medical magazine to learn more about DNA testing as we know it today through our DNA in our blood.

32
Bridge Over Troubled Waters

The silent, peaceful, calm of a Sunday afternoon was broken by the ringing of the telephone. My first reaction was not to answer it. It was time for my Sunday afternoon nap! However, upon answering the phone, I learned it was my longtime friend George, and thus I was quite happy to pick up the receiver.

However, upon hearing George's troubled voice, the calm nature of the afternoon ended. George said, "Ron, I need to talk with you privately." We agreed he would come over right away to my home.

George started by telling me that he had a tough and challenging week. George works for a large service provider company. He was feeling very unhappy and depressed about many aspects of his life. This past Wednesday, in particular, he was having a very challenging time concentrating at work. So, he decided at lunchtime; he would go for a walk. He walked for some time and eventually found himself on a bridge. He stood on the bridge, staring into the sky, and before long, he was standing on the railing. As he considered how unhappy he was, he decided that he would jump into the river and end it all. "Ron," George said, "Just as I was preparing to jump, your son Adam appeared."

When I gave George a strange and startled look, George said, "Yes, Ron, I am not kidding you; Adam appeared, and Adam said to me, George, don't jump! Adam said it three times! It was on that third time, 'George, don't jump' that Adam physically pulled me off the railing." After a long pause, George said, "Ron, Adam saved my life! Ron, your son saved my life. Ron, I just had to tell you."

George and I spoke several times over the next few months. We shared scripture and prayed together. At one point, George advised me that he was following up on my suggestion to have discussions with a local pastor. He also offered that if it were helpful, he would share his experiences with my sons, as he knew they were all struggling with the death of their brother Adam. George thought that since he saw Adam and that Adam spoke to him, it might give them some assurance that Adam was OK! To date, that conversation has not taken place.

In late 2018 I met George for breakfast. The intent of this meeting was the topic of writing this book. I provided him with some draft details to obtain his feedback. George indicated that periodically he still interacts with Adam; usually, it takes place while he is riding alone in his truck.

At this breakfast meeting, I also shared my gut-wrenching experience that I encountered with completing suicide. The timing of this experience was approximately three months after Adam's death. I received a call from Adam's wife, Maura, informing me that she had some items for me to pick up that were personal items belonging to Adam. Many items were papers, documents, college information, etc. Also, she said that she had two guns that were given to her by the coroner. Maura noted that one of the guns was used by Adam to complete suicide. Maura did not want the guns, and she wanted them out of her house.

Upon arriving at Maura's home, I looked through the boxes and then looked at the guns. Both were tagged by the coroner, noting name, case number, caliber, serial number, and DOD. As I was looking at the guns, I was praying, "What should I do with them?" After considering my options, I decided to take them. I loaded the guns and boxes into my car.

In looking through the boxes, I noted there wasn't any ammunition. I then proceeded to drive from Maura's home, through Mechanicsburg to Interstate 81. The further I drove, the more I thought about the "gun" in my car that took my son's life. I was approaching the area of the Silver Springs Mall when the thought hit me. "I could stop at a store, purchase some ammunition, drive up to the wooded area near Pine Grove Furnace, where Adam completed suicide and join him!"

Currently, with all the unresolved issues in my life, I was feeling quite depressed. The thought of death seemed like a quick and easy way out. However, the power of the Holy Spirit living in me since the age of twelve intervened! I began to remember the many truths as a Christian that I had available to me because of the GRACE of God! By accepting God's Riches At Christ's Expense, I had power over death and could eliminate the power of the Devil, who was attacking me at this time. Also, I thought about all the responsibilities that I currently had with my blended family. So, I proceeded to go north on Interstate 81 toward Halifax and prayed "all the way home!"

In some of my prior research, I learned that depression is one of the primary forces behind suicide. This information is summarized on the following pages. The information points out that we all have a DOB (Date of Birth) and a DOD (Date of Death). The "dash" represents the time that you are alive on this earth. For example, Adam's DOB is 01/06/1975, and his DOD is 09/11/2004. Adam's "dash" was twenty-nine years, eight months and five days

DOB—DOD.

Completing suicide will shorten the time available in a person's life where one can do things that will be classified as "Whats" coming out of "Whys." In my case, if I would have given in to the Devil and completed suicide, my legacy would have been cut short! Also, if my legacy would have been cut short, I would not be able to write this book, and thus those who will be able to benefit from the content of this writing would be deprived that opportunity!

GOD PROVIDED WISDOM

This is a good time for us to go back and be reminded of a very powerful verse:

2 Corinthians 4:8b: ". . . (TLB) we are perplexed because we don't know why things happen the way they do, but we don't give up and quit."

Live Life and Leave a Legacy
Old Testament - Joshua 23:1-10
Three things Joshua lived by (his legacy):
1. Be very Courageous, i.e., stand up for God.
2. Be very Cautious, i.e., continue to obey God's Laws.
3. Be very Constant, i.e., remain faithful to God.

Delight in God. Depend on God. Devote yourself to God.

Follow this outline, and no one will be able to stand against you— what a LEGACY!!

My prayer is that my dash (years working for the Lord) will be characterized as follows:

A. "I have fought a good fight, I have finished the course, and I have kept the faith."

B. When I am promoted to heaven, having God say to me, "Well done thou good and faithful servant."

C. Once in heaven, having people come up to me and say, "because of you, Ron, I am here in heaven."

Having the above outline characterize our "dash" will enable us to leave a fantastic LEGACY!!

CHALLENGE:

Consider what you would like your "dash" to represent. Complete the following statements:

1. When I stand before God in heaven, I would like to hear Him say to me:

_____

2. I defended His name when I:

_____

3. I fought a good fight; I kept the faith when I:

_____

33
Job Loss – Medical Challenges

In early 1998, I worked as a human resources professional for Keystone Financial. For many reasons, I was experiencing God's calling to a more active role in the Lay Ministry. This resulted in being hired by Halifax United Methodist Church as their Associate for Education and Youth Ministry effective July 1, 1998.

At this time, the *Patriot-News* had a weekly article titled *Meet Your Neighbor*. A reporter for this weekly article contacted me requesting an interview. Little did I know that a banking executive, who I used to work for, saw the article. The executive shared this article information with a West Point classmate of his who was in the process of starting an immigration processing business. They needed someone with a human resources background and thus eventually offered the position of Green Card Department Manager to me. I accepted effective July 1, 2000. The growth of the company, as well as the responsibility of my position, expanded rapidly.

For approximately a decade, I had what I considered the ideal set up. The owners were devout Christians who loved the Lord and ran their growing business in a Christ-like manner. Thus they respected my desire to be involved in the Lay Ministry work of Halifax United Methodist Church.

Unfortunately, due to an economic decline, company structure issues needed to be addressed in 2011. I was one of the individuals impacted when my job as Green Card Department Manager was eliminated. I was transferred to a newly created job, Administrator Manager, and advised that my annual salary would be lowered $10,000 in June 2011.

The year 2011 also held several far-reaching challenges for my family and me:

- My mother-in-law was promoted to heaven in April 2011.

- My father-in-law was promoted to heaven in May 2011.

- I was advised effective June 10, 2011, my job of Administrator Manager was being eliminated and I should proceed to file for unemployment compensation. The owners advised me that they needed to go deeper into the company with their cut-backs due to the continued faltering economy.

- I was diagnosed on June 30th with Parkinson's disease. This medical disorder involves the nervous system of the body. It typically progresses fairly quickly in attacking the body in movement inhibiting ways. So, I am a 63-year old male who has a very debilitating disease that has no known cure!

- I went to another neurologist in early July 2011 for a second opinion. The diagnosis was confirmed.

- My mother had to go under hospice care in September 2011. She was promoted to heaven!

- I developed other medical issues while medicating for Parkinson's disease: Venous Insufficiency, Spinal Stenosis, Lymphedema, shortness of breath, frequent nose bleeds, and a tumor removal from the pituitary gland in June 2017. At my spring 2020 annual MRI review, I learned that the tumor removed in June 2017 is showing signs of regrowth (I guess God has more hospital personnel for me to minister to.)

On one occasion, I expressed these medical problems to a Christian friend. He advised me to pray and seek God's help and faith to "grow old gracefully." I must admit that was not what I wanted to hear at that time. But over the passing years, I more and more see the wisdom in his comments!

For the first time in my life, I was relying upon many medications to restore good health even though many of the side effects were scary and unpredictable. For example, here is a classic: everyone in our home, including my wife and children, was sound asleep. Suddenly I heard a scratching noise coming from the far corner of our bedroom. I raucously opened one eye to survey the situation. Scanning our almost cave dark room, from the point of peering over ruffled sheets, was a considerable challenge. A period of time passed, which seemed like an eternity; suddenly, I saw a furry, large, creeping rodent. Being that I was not able to sit up and turn on the bedroom light, I had to wait for the creeping creature to pass through my window of visibility.

Eventually, the creepy creature stopped squarely in my line of sight. Now I was able to confirm that this furry, crawling creature was nothing more than the largest RAT I had ever seen.

Assuring myself that I was not dreaming, when really I was dreaming, I did not move a muscle in my entire body except my wide-open green eyeballs. Slowly but surely, the RAT followed the perimeter of our bedroom and dressing area and scratched and sniffed the baseboard as he moved along.

I began to try and wake my wife, but I was too scared to move; I was virtually paralyzed. However, I had to do something soon, as the RAT was approaching my side of our bedroom.

Fortunately, in my dream, which seemed so real, the RAT stopped to investigate a large dust ball under our bed. This dust ball was swaying slowly in the breeze created by our bedroom ceiling fan. This distracted the RAT and gave me the needed time to develop a plan.

I planned to remain still until the RAT was directly beside me. I would jump off the bed and surround him with both arms, eventually smothering him. In my dream, this plan seemed so realistic and very doable!

It was at this time that my wife was awakened from unusual noises that I was making. She observed me springing up into the air, curving my flight pattern out over the bedroom floor where I visualized (in my dream) the location of the RAT.

I was rudely awakened when I did a face plant onto our carpeted floor. Pat screamed, and I began to cry and laugh. Thank God I was not hurt; fortunately, I landed uncut between two pieces of sharp-cornered furniture.

Advancements in medicine have been fantastic in maintaining a reasonable quality of life while coping with the challenges of Parkinson's Disease. Some slow down the effects of the disease, while others address the current everyday discomforts associated with the disease. Dr. Mark Blakeslee, my neurologist since I was diagnosed with Parkinson's disease in mid-2011, has done and continues to do an excellent job balancing these issues in my case.

From a very practical standpoint, sometimes, God allows these experiences to take place so that we discover other positive outcomes. In discussing this experience with my doctor, I came to realize that one logical move on my part was simply to put my side of the bed against the wall.

Another medical related challenge that we experienced involved one of our sons. Kaleb, our next to the youngest son, was a junior at Halifax Area High School.

On this Maundy Thursday afternoon (Easter season for our schools), Halifax high school was hosting Newport High School in a varsity baseball game. The game was in the third inning. Kaleb was up to bat when he swung at a fastball on the inside part of the plate. The ball hit the bat and ricocheted back toward Kaleb's face striking him on the tibia on the right side of his mouth.

Kaleb dropped to his knees. The coach for Halifax ran to aid Kaleb as he began to spit blood on the ground and on home plate. Coach Bostorf asked me to come to Kaleb because his teeth were pointing in various directions. When I got to Kaleb I knelt beside him. The first thing that Kaleb mumbled to me was, "I'm going back into the game—I'm not sitting down."

I said to Kaleb, "stay here; the first thing we are going to do is pray."

After we finished praying, Kaleb, mom and I went to our local dentist's office. They could not help us as the injury was too sever; they indicated that surgery would probably be required. We then went to the local hospital emergency room to see the dentist who sometimes is on call and had been recommended to us by our local dentist. This recommended dentist was not on call that evening; however, he was located by cell phone at a local area restaurant. Since he had several social drinks with dinner, he excused himself from being considered to provide needed dental services to Kaleb.

The Orthodontist who was on call at the hospital that evening was contacted. It was amazing what this Orthodontist accomplished in his office without surgery. After repositioning the teeth (yes, it was quite painful) on the right/upper side of Kaleb's mouth, he placed special tape across the upper teeth. He also gave Kaleb a mouth piece to keep in his mouth at all times so he could keep upward pressure on the teeth. Amazing!

I wanted to let the Orthodontist know that I recognized how God had used him to help our son (always looking to plant spiritual seeds in the minds of others), so I said, "God really used you to help our son." In return, to my surprise, the orthodontist said, "thank you, however, also remember what He did for all of us in sending His Son to die for us (Good Friday is tomorrow).

We had a follow-up appointment with the Orthodontist on Easter Monday. The doctor approved the masks purchased for Kaleb to wear in future games. Kaleb then asked if he could play in the next high school game which was scheduled for the next day. Upon hearing this, Kaleb's mother almost "swallowed her gum".

The Orthodontist said he was an athlete in high school and college and he understood Kaleb's desire to remain in the line-up. Also, he felt the quality of the masks was such that they would provide the protection he needed to further protect him from injury.

Tuesday, the game was at Upper Dauphin area high school in Elizabethville, Pennsylvania (a very tough/talented team who is one of our strongest opponents). My wife and I were about 10 minutes late in arriving at the game. We were virtually certain that Adam would not play in this game because of his injury and we had several pressing items to complete at home.

When we arrived at the stadium, everyone was very excited. We were told something we could hardly believe; not only did Adam start in the game, the first time up to bat in the top of the first inning, Kaleb hit a home run over the center field fence! God is amazing!

GOD PROVIDED WISDOM

This experience made real for me the fact that the devil and his demons are constantly at work in trying to discourage me in any way possible. The devil knows he has lost me to Christ; however, he also knows if he can make my testimony weak, that will limit the spread of my faith to others and make me less effective in making disciples for Jesus Christ.

2 Corinthians 1:3-5 (TLB): "What a wonderful God we have—He is the Father of our Lord Jesus Christ, the source of every mercy, and the one who so wonderfully comforts and strengthens us in our hardships and trials. And why does He do this? So that when others are troubled, needing our sympathy and encouragement, we can pass on to them this same help and comfort God has given us."

2 Corinthians 4:8b (TLB): The Apostle Paul states, "We are perplexed because we don't know why things happen as they do, but we don't give up and quit."

Psalm 91:1-2 (TLB): "We live within the shadow of the Almighty, sheltered by the God who is above all gods. This I declare, that He alone is my refuge, my place of safety; He is my God, and I am trusting him."

CHALLENGE:
Looking at the three verses above, which one provides you with the most peace of mind and reassurance?

____ 2 Corinthians 1:3-5 ____ 2 Corinthians 4:8b ____ Psalm 91:1-2

Why? _____

34
Witnessing During Life Challenges

In 2017 issues surfaced regarding the clarity of my vision. An eye specialist discovered a Suparsalas Lesion (liquid-filled tumor) attached to the stalk of my pituitary gland. As this tumor grew, optic nerve pressure negatively impacted my vision.

The power of the Holy Spirit enabled me to have peace of mind regarding this finding. My focus to God was, "what do you want to accomplish through these events?" Almost immediately, the idea of producing a witnessing card for distribution came to mind. The final product was a laminated, two-sided document.

This document was initially designed to give to persons who visit me in the hospital. Thus the reason the card begins by saying, "Take this card with you ..." However, it wasn't long until the Holy Spirit revealed to me that the cards should be given to hospital personnel who provide services to me. Therefore my approach was as follows: "When a person is in the hospital, it is common practice for friends and relatives to send them a card wishing them a speedy recovery. I have decided to turn the tables and give a card to them who visit or provide medical services.

During my nine days in the hospital, I distributed all 44 cards. All attempts to deliver a card in this manner were successful except in one case where a nurse refused the offer.

Card distribution did not stop with my discharge. I was able to share the cards with a physical therapy trainee, a SEARS's repairman and trainee, a Pennsylvania State Trooper investigating an auto accident, and the

Chaplin of the Chicago Cubs major league baseball team. And the distribution continues.

GOD PROVIDED WISDOM

Side one of the card reads as follows:

> Thanks for Coming! (visitor or hospital employee) Take this info with you:
>
> Isaiah 40:31 (KJV):
> But they that wait upon the Lord shall renew their strength. They shall mount up with wings like eagles; they shall run and not be weary; they shall walk and not faint.
>
> Ephesians 5:15-17 (TLB):
> So be careful how you act; these are difficult days. Don't be fools; be wise: make the most of every opportunity you have for doing good. Do not act thoughtlessly but try to find out and do whatever the Lord wants you to.
>
> James 1:6 (TLB) :
> But when you ask Him (God), be sure that you really expect him to tell you, for a doubtful mind will be as unsettled as a wave of the sea that is driven and tossed by the wind.

Side two of the card reads as follow:

2016 World Series Ring

Jesus conquered the grave

The death and resurrection of Jesus proved that the grave has been conquered. Salvation is a gift from God, unlike a World Series ring that has to be earned.

- God loves us—John 3:16

- All are contaminated with sin—Romans 3:16

- All are dead unto sin—Romans 6:23

- Christ died for all who accept Him as Savior—Romans 5:6-8

- All can be saved who believe in Jesus as the Son of God—Acts16:30-31

- A person can be saved and know it—1 John 5:10-13

- Once a child of God, a person should have a desire to obey Him—Acts 5:29

CHALLENGE:

Which passage on the previous page speaks the most to you? Why?

35
Many Blessings Through It All

I, like many other professing Christians, look to the apostle Paul as one of the great contributors to our faith. He made a great switch when he changed from the persecutor of Christians to becoming a dedicated follower of Jesus himself.

This conversion of Paul is a neat example of how God saw Paul, not for whom he was but what he could become. I see this so vividly when reading the many letters that Paul wrote to the early Christians.

As I come to a close in sharing my story of how God worked in my life for His glory, many people come to mind. I like to think of it as "through it all, there were still many blessings—some obvious and some not so obvious."

For starters, look at Marion. As she sought forgiveness for earlier sins, she did an excellent job of demonstrating to Drew a desire to get right with God. By seeking forgiveness, and my willingness to extend such forgiveness, illustrated the basic concept of Christian love, i.e. seeking and giving forgiveness.

My three older children (Bryan, Heather, Adam) were somewhat reserved in accepting Pat as my future wife and their future step-mother. This came out in a session we (Pat, Bryan, Heather, Adam, and me) had behind closed doors just prior to our wedding. They were unsure who Pat would "become" as their step-mother. Yet through the power of prayer and thus through intervention of the Holy Spirit, today we are a close family, interacting often and sharing acts of love.

At the time of Adam's death many people were upset and frustrated with his decision to end his life, even if it was under duress caused by mental illness. Today the focus is on the Adam as described by his college coach, i.e., "when off the football field he was like a big teddy bear, however when on the football field he was like a bear with a sore butt."

Also, many "whats" have resulted as we share Adam's story; I'm sure that was God's intention. Today, as your reading of this book comes to a close, let me ask you:

- Who are you becoming?

- Do you know Jesus as the Lord of your life?

- Are you leaning on Jesus when in need or are you relying on your own skills?

- Is the Holy Spirit active in your life daily?

- If the Holy Spirit is active in your life daily, who are you "becoming" through the use of this power?

Remember, Moses killed a man and yet through the power of forgiveness, God used him in fantastic ways. Also, the thief on the cross sinned often, yet Jesus promised that He would see him in Paradise because of his desire to be forgiven. Likewise, you and I have sinned, yet through Christ's victory in conquering the grave, we too can have a glorious time in heaven one day with Jesus and all others who put their faith and trust in Him!

GOD PROVIDED WISDOM

God sees us not as who we were but who we can become through the Power of the Holy Spirit. He sees us as persons who will be willing to work on the "whats" that need to be accomplished. However, many times we lack motivation to get involved in the action.

Remember: the death and resurrection of Jesus proved that the grave has been conquered. Many times, when dealing with this subject, we have good intentions, but we don't let the Holy Spirit work through us. Most times it requires stepping out in faith in order to accomplish the "whats" that God has in mind for us.

As a young boy President John F. Kennedy loved to hear stories about his grandfather's boyhood in Ireland. Grandfather Fitzgerald used to walk home from school with a group of youngsters each day. The boys would sometimes taunt each other to climb over the stone walls along the lanes of the countryside. Young Fitzgerald and the other boys were sometimes hesitant to dare the hazardous climbs. However, they devised a way to motivate themselves to take the risk involved. They would toss their hats over the wall. They knew that they dare not go home without their hats. Thus, they motivated themselves to make the treacherous climb over the walls.

There are times when we need to toss our hats over the wall. We see where there is something that God wants us to do. Or, we note that someone desperately needs help but yet we're not willing to take that step of faith and get involved. Also, there are the times when the "whats" are things like changing jobs, starting a new business, moving into a new part of town, going back to college, etc. There come those times in life when we feel the need to make a change.

I am reminded of one young man, thirty years of age, who made such a change. He had been successful in the small business that had been left to him by his father. He was liked and respected by his friends and neighbors. He was meeting his responsibilities. But he knew that this was not where he belonged. He was called to a ministry; i.e., a ministry of teaching and preaching and healing. And thus, he threw his hat over the wall! At first he met with spectacular success. His reputation spread with amazing speed. But as his popularity increased, so did the number of his critics. Particularly in his own hometown did he meet with hostility. Some of his closest friends came quietly to try to silence him. They were afraid, as they put it, saying that he was "beside" himself. Even his own family was concerned. But he persevered in his new calling for three years, only to die an untimely death. As he hung on a tree between two thieves, feeling forsaken by both God and man, no one would have judged his life a success. But it was! He conquered the grave!

Sometimes, as in Jesus's case, it is those closest to us who have the hardest time coming to grips with our dreams and aspirations that relate to the "whats" that God is calling us to accomplish.

There comes a time when we must toss our hat over the wall even though we know we will have our critics. Nothing is ever accomplished by persons who value comfort and safety above all else. There comes a time for what is often called a leap of faith!

However, the greatest adventure that one can start out on—the most spectacular and often the most courageous change that can be made in a life, is that of becoming a Disciple of Jesus Christ. By asking God to forgive our sins and be our Savior and thus be filled with the Holy Spirit, we will one day be in heaven. In the meantime we can assist God in accomplishing the "Whats" that need to be accomplished, i.e. making disciples for Jesus Christ; REMEMBER:

- John 3:16 (God loves you)
- Romans 3:23 (All are sinners)
- Romans 6:23 (All are dead in sin)
- Romans 5:6-8 (Jesus Christ died for you and me)
- Acts 16;30-31 (We can be saved by faith in Jesus)
- 1 John 5:10-13 (We can be saved and know it)
- Acts 5:29 (Once saved, child of God, have desire to obey HIM)

CHALLENGE:

Write down two situations where you need to "Toss your hat over the wall" so that you are motivated to get things moving. Then through prayer and Bible reading, put your plans into motion. Remember that when you add the letter "W" to "hat" you get "What."

Then watch "What" the "What team" will accomplish!

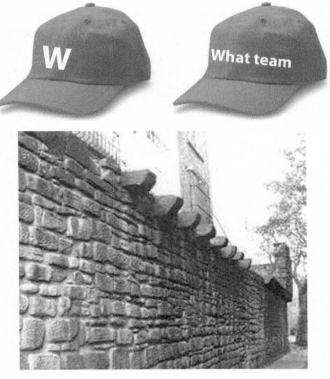

By being "motivated" you can be a member of the "What Team" and accomplish one of the "Whats" that God wanted done; all you have to do is throw your hat over the perceived wall and put your "Faith and Trust" in God!

Epilogue

A review of Chinese history reveals information of a deadly virus (Coronavirus) that originated in China and quickly made its way to the USA. This event caused great concern across our nation and consumed the time and effort of our president, as well as virtually impacting every citizen of our country in one way or another.

As expected from an event like this, all kinds of "Why" questions surface:

- Why has God allowed this virus to be created?

- Why has God allowed all this confusion and uncertainty to evolve because it takes the focus of Christians away from worshiping and honoring God?

- Why has God allowed this interruption and thus have the focus on an Invisible Enemy (Coronavirus) rather than God's Invisible Love (Saving Grace)?

- Why hasn't God allowed our laboratory personnel to have more timely success in developing a vaccine to use in battling this virus?

- Etc.

After considering many "Why" questions, my thoughts shifted to "What" questions, i.e. what does God want to accomplish through me as a result of the introduction of this virus into our environment?

I began to think about all the people in the world who are lost as it relates to God's saving grace (many of these points were identified in the book you just read). Many times it takes a catestroic event to get the attention of those who never made an affirmative response to God's call to be saved. In the case of Coronavirus, everyone is impacted. The virus can't be seen (the Invisible Enemy), yet has a potentially devastating result; it captures the attention of everyone.

Also, recognize that God's saving grace is invisible. However, if not accepted, and thus not having God reside within us in the form of the Holy Spirit, the Bible conveys that we will spend eternity in Hell (a real place, potentially far worse than acquiring the Coronavirus). Therefore, if the Coronavirus causes an unsaved person to accept Jesus as the Master of his life, this is a tremendous result. Thus any part I can play in this process is an excellent outcome from my "What" question efforts!

I heard of a lady named Sally who was having difficulty understanding the way of God's saving grace. She simply could not understand what it meant to receive Jesus as her Savior. When she told her pastor about her dilemma, he asked her a question: "What is your last name?" When she answered "Jones", he asked, "How long has your name been Jones?" "Ever since my husband and I were married 35 years ago," She answered. The pastor than said, "How did you become Mrs. Jones?" "It happened at the wedding," she replied. "The pastor asked me, 'Will you have this man to be your lawful wedded husband?' And I said yes."

The pastor went on to say, "In your answering of the pastor's questions, didn't you say, 'I'd like to—or—I hope to—or—I'll try to take him as my husband?'" "No," the woman answered. "I said I will, and that is all there was to it!" The pastor said, "God wants you to take Jesus as your Savior. What should you respond to His question regarding taking Jesus as your Savior forever?" The lady said "I will—how simple!"

Throughout this book (Why vs What), many examples have been provided that demonstrate the power our God maintains. Thus, when other challenges like the Coronavirus surface, remember God is in control and focus on "What" does God want to accomplish through me?" With my focus on this question, coupled with the acceptance of God's saving grace offered through the death and resurrection of His Son Jesus (see Sally's story above), one day God will say to me in heaven "Well done thou good and faithful servant, you focused on the "What" and not the "Why!"

Appendix A
Precious Memories

Adam and Kaleb, following the Bloomsburg vs. Millersville game in October 1996.

Following are a few examples received on the day Adam's Celebration of Life service:

"I will always remember Adam's brown eyes, big smile and his love for football and baseball. I was always proud of the fact he graduated from Bloomsburg University and played college football - the sport he so loved. His being a Parole Officer was also quite an accomplishment that I'll never forget! Thanks for the memories, Adam." —*Nancy Bastian*

"So many great memories! The ring bearer at our wedding. The night of our rehearsal he was bouncing off the walls. He was hiding back in the church pews. Our "BIG" nephew, the football player. I loved to watch you play (and very proud too!). Your hearty laugh at all our family gets togethers. Coming to w' boro to play golf with Jordan and me. Teasing Jordan about shooting an eleven point buck (really a spike). We miss you so much!!!"

—Uncle Eric & Aunt Judy

"In my years of growing up with Adam my best and most fond memory is playing baseball with him. Numerous times we would practice throwing the ball back and forth to each other. I will always remember playing with the best player on my team."

—Jason Bastian

"I am Adam's Grandpa Reitz. Adam used to sit on my lap and drive the lawn tractor. When he grew up and went to college, I helped him build a bunk bed and desk in his dormitory."

—C. Arthur Reitz

Etc.

Appendix B
The Singing Benediction

To be used at the Celebration of Life Service for Ron Reitz; date: Unknown.

Benediction sung to the tune of "I've Got a Home in Glory Land"

I've got a home in Glory land that outshines the sun;
I've got a home in Glory land that outshines the sun;
I've got a home in Glory land that outshines the sun;
Way beyond the blue!

I loved planting seeds; for the Lord;
I loved planting seeds; for the Lord;
I loved planting seeds; for the Lord;
Now I see the Fruit!

I've got baseball up in heaven; yes I do;
I've got baseball up in heaven; yes I do;
I've got baseball up in heaven; yes I do;
Hitting many home runs!

I've got cherry pie up in heaven;
I've got cherry pie up in heaven;
I've got cherry pie up in heaven;
Pie a la mode

I love playing board games; up in heaven;
I love playing board games; up in heaven;
I love playing board games; up in heaven;
Where no one cheats!

I took Jesus as my Savior, you take Him too;
I took Jesus as my Savior, you take Him too;
I took Jesus as my Savior, you take Him too;
While He's calling you!

Appendix C
95 Facts

95 Facts about Art and his life (example facts listed)

1. Clair Arthur Reitz came into this world on January 29, 1920.

2. Arthur was the first born child of Ellis and Maude Reitz. He preferred the name Arthur (Art) when he was growing up. He has always signed his name, C. Arthur Reitz.

3. Art had two sisters, Goldie and Betty. Betty died in infancy.

4. Art's father worked for the Pennsylvania Railroad.

5. Art was born and grew up in the town of Sunbury in Northumberland County Pennsylvania.

6. Art and his family lived in various locations in Sunbury: Court Street where he was born; Reagan Street; Fairnount Avenue; and on the corner of East Chestnut and Tenth Streets. His parents would buy a house, remodel and/or repair it and then resell it for a profit.

7. After leaving the home on Chestnut and Tenth Streets, the family moved to a farm at R. D. #3 Sunbury.

8. Art attended the Drumheller School for first and second grades.

9. Etc.—until you have 95 facts.

Thank You from Author

THANK YOU to many friends and family for their support in making this book a reality. A special thank you to my son Landon for his writing insights and skills!

—Ron Reitz, Author

About the Author

Ron Reitz is a devout Christian dedicated to spreading God's word. As a Certified Lay Minister (CLM), Reitz's approach is to plant seeds of truth into believers' minds and wait for watering and harvest. By staying in close contact with God through prayer and Bible reading, he continues to receive direction from God and to continue forward on his path to righteousness. He lives in Halifax, Pennsylvania.

Made in the USA
Monee, IL
19 August 2020